# Biography of an American Bondman by His Daughter

# Biography of an American Bondman by His Daughter

Josephine Brown

*Biography of an American Bondman by His Daughter* was first published in 1855.

This edition published by Mint Editions 2020.

ISBN 9781513278667 | E-ISBN 9781513279121

Published by Mint Editions®

minteditionbooks.com

Publishing Director: Jennifer Newens
Design & Production: Rachel Lopez Metzger
Project Manager: Micaela Clark
Typesetting: Westchester Publishing Services

*"THEY who sell mothers by the pound, and children in lots to suit purchasers—what are they? I care not what terms are applied to them, provided they DO apply. If they are not thieves, if they are not tyrants, if they are not men stealers, I should like to know what is their true character, and by what names they may be called."*

—WILLIAM LLOYD GARRISON

*"LET us not require too much of slavery.*

*Let us not insist that the slaves shall never be separated, nor their families broken up,"*

—NEHEMIAH ADAMS, D. D.

# Contents

| | |
|---|---:|
| Preface | 9 |
| I | 11 |
| II | 15 |
| III | 17 |
| IV | 19 |
| V | 20 |
| VI | 22 |
| VII | 24 |
| VIII | 26 |
| IX | 28 |
| X | 30 |
| XI | 32 |
| XII | 35 |
| XIII | 37 |
| XIV | 42 |
| XV | 43 |
| XVI | 47 |
| XVII | 48 |

| | |
|---|---|
| XVIII | 52 |
| XIX | 56 |
| XX | 57 |
| XXI | 62 |
| XXII | 67 |
| XXIII | 72 |
| XXIV | 75 |

# Preface

*While at school in France, I was often beset by my fellow students to know the history of my father, whom they heard was a fugitive from American despotism. To satisfy their curiosity, I wrote out the first ten chapters of the following pages, as I had heard the incidents related. On returning to America last August, and finding that the narrative of my father's life, written by him, and published some years ago, was out of print, I determined to supply its place; and therefore have added a few more chapters to those written while abroad.*

Josephine Brown

# I

*"Rouse ye, and break the massive chain,*
*The fetter'd slave that binds;*
*And check the sorrow and the pain*
*The wretched negro finds."*

Five different biographies of the subject of the following pages have been published, during the last seven years,—two in the United States and three in Great Britain. Of these, one was translated into German, and appeared in Dresden, and another was published in the French language in Paris. The writer of this, however, fancies that the relation which she holds to the author of "Sketches Of Places And People Abroad," gives her an advantage over those who have preceded her.

William Wells Brown was born on the farm of Dr. John Young, near Lexington, Kentucky, on the 15th of March, 1815. His father's name was George Higgins, half brother to Dr. Young. The Doctor removed to the State of Missouri, and took with him William and his mother, the former being then an infant. Dr. Young located himself in the interior of the State, sixty miles above St. Louis, in a beautiful and fertile valley, a mile from the river. A finer situation for a farm could scarcely have been selected in any part of the country. With a climate favorable to agriculture, and soil rich, the most splendid crops of tobacco, hemp, flax and grain were produced on the new plantation. On this farm, Elizabeth (William's mother) was put to work at field service. Distinguished for her strength both of body and mind, and a woman of great courage, Elizabeth was considered one of the most valuable slaves on the place. Although Dr. Young was not thought to be the hardest of masters, he nevertheless employed, as an overseer, a man whose acts of atrocity could scarcely have been surpassed in any of the slave States. Grove Cook was a large, tall man, with rough features, red hair, grey eyes, and large, bushy eyebrows, which gave his face the appearance of a spaniel dog. Like most negro drivers, Cook was addicted to drunkenness, and when the least intoxicated, would use the whip without mercy upon those with whom he came in contact. This was the man selected by Dr. Young to look after his plantation, and superintend its affairs.

William was separated from his mother at an early age, and was but seldom allowed to see her. The young slave was taught by bitter experience the want of a mother's care and softening influence. At the age of eight years, he was taken into his master's medical office, and was employed in tending upon the Doctor. As William grew older, he became more serviceable in his new situation. When only about ten years old, the tender feelings of the young slave were much hurt at hearing the cries and screams of his mother, and seeing the driver flogging her with his negro-whip. As he heard the loud, sharp crack of the lash, and the groans of her who was near and dear to him, William felt a cold chill run through his veins. He wept bitterly, but could render no assistance. What could be more heart-rending than to see a dear and beloved one abused without being able to give her the slightest aid? Overseers at the South generally pride themselves upon their ability to break the stubborn spirit of the negro; and the man who shall suffer a slave, male or female, to disobey a rule, without being able to flog him or her for such disobedience, would be immediately discharged by the proprietor. Ability to manage a negro is the first qualification for a good slave-driver. The Doctor had, among his fifty slaves, a man named Randall, of stout frame, and more than six feet in height, and known as the most powerful slave on the farm. If there was heavy work to be done, Randall was always selected to do it; and his task was sure to be finished before any other person's. The Doctor had flogged every slave on the place but Randall, and he would willingly have whipped him, but that he feared the undertaking, for Randall had often been heard to say, "No white man shall ever whip me; I will die first." Cook, from the time that he came upon the plantation, had frequently declared that he could and would flog any nigger that was put into the field to work under him.

Doctor Young having been elected to represent his district in the State Legislature, Cook took the entire management of the plantation. The Doctor had repeatedly told him not to attempt to whip Randall, but he was determined to try it. As soon as he was sole dictator, he thought the time had come to put his threats into execution. He soon began to find fault with Randall, and threatened to whip him if he did not do better. One day he gave him a very hard task,—more than he could possibly do,—and at night, the task not being performed, he told Randall that he should remember him the next morning.

On the following morning, after the hands had taken breakfast, Cook called out Randall and told him that he intended to whip him, and ordered him to cross his hands and be tied. The slave asked why he wished to whip him. He answered, because he had not finished his task the day previous. Randall said his task was too great, or he should have done it. Cook said it made no difference, he should whip him. The slave stood silent for a moment, and then said—"Mr. Cook, I have always tried to please you since you have been on the plantation, and I find that you are determined not to be pleased or satisfied with my work, let me do as well as I may. No man has laid hands on me to whip me for the last ten years, and I have long since come to the conclusion not to be whipped by any man living." Cook, finding by Randall's looks and gestures that he would resist, called three of the hands from their work, and commanded them to seize the insolent slave and tie him. The men stood still; they knew their fellow-slave to be a powerful man, and were afraid to grapple with him. As soon as Cook had ordered them to seize him, Randall turned to them and said—"Boys, you all know me; you know I can handle any three of you; and the man that lays hands on me shall die. This white man can't whip me himself, and therefore he has called you to help him." The overseer was unable to prevail upon them to aid him, and finally ordered them to go to their work.

Nothing was said to Randall by the overseer for more than a week. One morning, however, while the hands were at work in the field, he came into it, accompanied by three friends of his,—Thompson, Woodbridge, and Jones. They came up to where Randall was at work, and Cook ordered him to leave and go with them to the barn. He refused to go; whereupon he was attacked by the overseer and his companions, when he turned upon them, and laid them one after another prostrate before him. Woodbridge drew out his pistol and fired at him, and brought him to the ground. The others rushed upon him with their clubs, and beat him over the head and face until they succeeded in tying him. He was then taken to a barn and tied to a beam. Cook gave him above one hundred lashes with a heavy cowhide, had his wounds washed with salt and water, and left him tied during the night. The next day, he was untied, and taken to a blacksmith's shop, and had a ball and chain attached to his leg. He was compelled to labor in the field, and perform the same amount of work other hands did.

When the Doctor returned home, he was pleased to find that Randall had been subdued in his absence, and highly praised the overseer for his good qualities as a negro-breaker.

The negro quarters were situated some distance from the master's mansion, or "great house," as it was called. The cabins were built of wood, with only one room, and no floor. The owner seldom provides bed and bedding for his slave, unless merely to give each one a coarse blanket; and those who are so fortunate as to get more than this, think themselves luxurious livers. The blowing of the horn and the ringing of the bell were the signals for Dr. Young's slaves to start in the morning to their daily toil, which lasted from twelve to fourteen hours. Being employed either as house servant, or in his master's medical department, William was exempt from the call of the horn and bell. Nevertheless, his life was a hard one. Nearly related to the Doctor, Mrs. Young was always punishing the young slave for some supposed offence, which, after all, was only because she felt angry and humiliated at the idea of having her husband's "negro relations" in her sight. The nearer a slave approaches an Anglo-Saxon in complexion, the more he is abused by both owner and fellow-slaves. The owner flogs him to keep him "in his place," and the slaves hate him on account of his being whiter than themselves. Thus the complexion of the slave becomes a crime, and he is made to curse his father for the Anglo-Saxon blood that courses through his veins.

If there is one evil connected with the abominable system of slavery which should be loathed more than another, it is taking from woman the right of self-defence, and making her subject to the control of any licentious villain who may be able to purchase her person. But amalgamation is only one of the impure branches which flow from this poisonous stream.

## II

> *"Waft, waft, ye winds, his story,*
> *And you, ye waters, roll,*
> *Till, like a sea of glory,*
> *It spreads from pole to pole."*

On Dr. Young's leaving home the second time, to attend the State Legislature, William was taken from his master's office and placed under Cook, the negro-driver, to work in the field. Not more than twelve years of age, and of a tender constitution, he found his new situation a most unpleasant and difficult one to fill. Seeing William neatly dressed and doing light work about the office, the overseer had often expressed a wish to have the "white nigger" under his charge. "I will tan your yellow jacket for you," said the negro-driver, as William took his hoe and followed the other slaves to the field. It was with pain that Elizabeth saw her son in the hands of this drunken man. William had been in the field scarcely a week, when Cook, for a pretended offence, took the young slave to the barn, tied him up, and inflicted a severe whipping upon him. In vain the mother pleaded for her child, and reminded the overseer that the boy was too young to perform the heavy labors given to him.

In punishing the slaves, the overseer was always inventing new modes of chastisement. On one occasion, Cook, in a fit of anger, because William did not keep up with the older hands in hoeing, gave the boy a flogging, and then took him into a pasture, where the sheep were grazing, and made him got down on his hands and knees in front of an old ram, noted for his butting qualities. As soon as the ram saw the boy in the butting attitude, he prepared himself for a fight, and, squaring off, he gave a bleat, and sprang forward, hitting William in the forehead, and knocking him upon the ground. The wound inflicted upon the poor boy caused the blood to gush from his nose. The overseer, and a few of his friends who were present to see the fun, laughed heartily, and the boy was sent back to work.

In the Doctor's absence, Cook ruled the slaves with an iron hand, using the negro-whip on all occasions where he was the least provoked. On the return of the Doctor from the Legislature, William was again removed from the field to his master's office.

Dr. Young was, without doubt, one of the most religious men south of "Mason and Dixon's line." He had family worship every night and morning, and on Sabbath morning, he spent an hour in reading and explaining Scripture to the blacks. If he punished a slave, he did it religiously. Quotations from the Bible, and a moral lecture, always accompanied the whip. "Servants, obey your masters," was continually on the Doctor's tongue. "He that knoweth his master's will, and doeth it not, shall be beaten with many stripes," was a part of his moral lecture to his slaves.

# III

*"Tell the man who dares to barter*
*In his brother's flesh and blood,*
*He has broken the high charter*
*Of our common brotherhood!"*

Dr. Young removed from the interior of Missouri, when William was thirteen years old, to St. Louis, where he purchased a farm of three thousand acres of land, within four miles of the city. Here he employed an overseer named Haskell, who was scarcely less cruel than Cook. William, however, was let out to Major Freeland, an inn-keeper in St. Louis. Freeland was from Virginia, and claimed to be one of the aristocracy of the Old Dominion. The Major was a horse-racer, gambler, cock-fighter, and was occasionally drunk, and would then rave about like a madman. When in these fits, he would take up a chair and throw it at any of the servants who came in his way. William had been with Freeland but a few weeks, when the Major tied the young slave up in the smoke-house, after whipping him severely, and caused him to be smoked with tobacco, the boy sneezing, coughing and weeping during this fiendish act.

William ran away, and went home and told his master of his ill treatment by Freeland. Instead of the Doctor sympathizing with his nephew, he flogged the boy, and sent him back to his employer. Fearing another punishment from the drunken in-keeper, William ran away and remained in the woods. But there he was not long safe, for some negro-hunters, with their dogs, came along, and the animals were soon on the scent of the young fugitive, who was captured, after taking refuge in a tree, and again returned to his master, Major Freeland. William received another flogging, and after being once more smoked, was again put to work.

After remaining with this monster for some months, the young and friendless slave-boy was hired out as a servant on one of the steamers running between St. Louis and Galena. Here he was first impressed with a love for freedom. As he saw others going from place to place, and using the liberty that God endowed every human being with, he pined to be as free as those who moved about him. Being at St. Louis on the Fourth of July, William had an opportunity of hearing an oration from the Hon. Thomas Hart Benton. The boy's young heart leaped with enthusiasm as he listened to the burning eloquence of "Old Bullion." It is a dangerous thing to permit a slave to hear these July orations; it kindles a feeling in favor of freedom which can never be effaced. It was so with William. "We hold these truths to be self-evident: that all men are created equal; that they are endowed by their Creator with certain unalienable rights; that among these are life, liberty, and the pursuit of happiness; that to secure these rights, governments are instituted among men, deriving their just powers from the consent of the governed,"—said the Senator, in concluding his speech; and these words, quoted from our Declaration of Independence, were indelibly impressed on the heart of this uneducated boy. In his sleep, he dreamed of freedom; when awake, his thoughts were about liberty, and how he could secure it.

From the moment that William heard the speech of Mr. Benton, he resolved that he would be free, and to this early determination, the cause of human freedom is indebted for one of its most effective advocates.

At the close of the summer, the boy was again taken home to the Doctor's plantation, and put to work in the field under Haskell, the overseer. The change was so great, that William wilted down under the hot sun, and the hard work given to him by the driver. The poor slave experienced all that the house servant must go through, on being transferred from the cabin of a steamer, or the master's mansion, to the rough labors of the field.

# IV

> *"What! mothers from their children riven?*
> *What! God's own image bought and sold?*
> *Americans to market driven,*
> *And bartered, as the brutes, for gold?"*

Speculation and mismanagement had so far reduced the Doctor's finances, that he found himself compelled to sell some of his slaves to repair his affairs, and Elizabeth, William's mother, was among the first that were sold. William had three brothers, who, together with his mother, were taken to the St. Louis negro market, and sold to the highest bidder. The boys were purchased by a slave-trader, and sent off to the lower country; but the mother was more fortunate, and became the slave of Isaac Mansfield, a gentleman residing in the city of St. Louis. The last tidings that William had of his brothers was, that they had been bought by a planter, and sent to his farm on the Yazoo River. If still living, they are lingering out a miserable existence on a cotton, sugar, or rice plantation, in a part of the country where the life of the slave has no parallel in deeds of atrocity. Nothing can be worse than slavery in Louisiana and Mississippi, on the banks of the noblest river in the world. A ride down that beautiful stream on one of the western floating palaces, causes one's heart to ache at seeing humanity so degraded. The rich plantations, waving with green and golden crops of cane, are interspersed here and there by a cotton plantation, with intervals of untrodden forests hanging over the banks, showing Nature in her most luxuriant state. Nothing can exceed the grandeur and beauty of the land thus cursed by the foul system of negro slavery. Truly may it be said, that this outrageous and unnatural institution has monopolized the best soil and finest climate in the New World.

## V

*"For now the ripened cane*
*Was ready for the knife,*
*And not a slave could be spared to aid*
*His mother or his wife."*

In the cotton districts, the picking season is always the most severe for the bondman, for when they gather in the cotton, the slaves are worked from fifteen to twenty hours out of the twenty-four. The sugar-making season commences about the middle or last of October, and continues from four to ten weeks, according to the season and other circumstances; but more especially, the number of hands on the plantation, and the amount of sugar to be made. As soon as the cane is ready for harvesting, the grinding-mill is got in order, wood hauled, the boiling-house cleaned out, the kettles scoured, the coolers caulked, and the casks arranged to receive the sugar. Before the cane is gathered in, plants, or sprouts, as they are sometimes called, are secured for the next season. This is done by cutting cane and putting it in matelas,— or mattressing it, as it is commonly denominated. The cane is cut and thrown into different parcels in the field, in quantities sufficient to plant several acres, and so placed that the tops of one layer may completely cover and protect the stalks of another. When the required amount is thus obtained, the whole gang of slaves is employed in cutting cane and taking it to the mill. The top is first cut from the cane, and then the stalks cut as close to the ground as possible, thrown into carts, or taken on the backs of mules to the grinding-house. As soon as it reaches the mill, it is twice passed between iron rollers, so that not a particle of juice is left in the stalk, the former passing into vats, or receivers, while the trash is thrown into carts, and conveyed from the mill and burned. After the juice is pressed from the cane, it is put into boilers, and transferred from one to another, until it reaches the last kettle, or teach, as it is termed. The sugar has then attained the granulating point, and is thus conveyed into the coolers, which hold between two and three hogsheads. It is then removed to the draining-house, after remaining twenty-four hours in the coolers, and soon after is put into the hogsheads. Here it undergoes the process of draining for five or six days, and is then ready for the market. A second-rate sugar is always made, after the first-class is manufactured.

During the whole of this process, the driver is never seen without a short-handled whip in his hand. The lash of the negro-whip is from four to six feet in length, made of cowhide, and sometimes wire plaited in with the leather. The handle of the whip, or the butt, is not unfrequently loaded or filled with lead.

Such is the process through which the sugar has to pass before it finds its way upon the tables of the people of the free States. William shrank back at the thought of his brothers dragging out their lives upon a cotton or sugar plantation.

## VI

*"A bitter smile was on her cheek,*
*And a dark flash in her eye."*

After remaining on the farm for a few weeks, under the iron rule of the overseer, William was again hired out to the proprietors of the steamer "Enterprise." On the second trip of the boat's return from Galena, she took on board, at Hannibal, a noted slave-trader, named Walker, who had with him between fifty and sixty slaves, consisting chiefly of men and women adapted to field service. In this gang of slaves, however, was a young woman, apparently about twenty years of age, with blue eyes, straight brown hair, prominent features, and perfectly white, with no indication whatever that a drop of African blood coursed through her veins. In describing this girl, in the published narrative of his life, Mr. Brown says:—"The woman attracted universal attention; but it was not so much the fairness of her complexion that created such a sensation among those who gazed upon her finely chiselled features; it was her almost unequalled beauty. She had been on board but a short time, before both ladies and gentlemen left their easy chairs to view the white slave. Throughout the day, the topic of conversation was the beautiful slave girl." This young woman was the daughter of a slaveholder, by one of his mulatto servants. Much anxiety was felt among the passengers to learn the history of this beautiful and innocent creature. The trader kept near her all the time. On the arrival of the boat at St. Louis, the gang, including the white slave, was removed to another steamer, bound for New Orleans, and the speculator, no doubt, on reaching the place of his destination, sold this American daughter for a high price, on account of her personal charms.

The steamer soon after being laid up for the remainder of the season, William was once more taken home, and employed as a house servant and carriage-driver. It was while acting in this capacity, that a deed of cruelty was committed, which is graphically described by Mr. Brown in his published narrative. While driving his master's carriage to church one Sabbath morning, he saw Mr. D. D. Page, with whom he was well acquainted, chasing one of his slaves round the yard, cutting him at every jump with a long negro-whip. Mr. Page, seeing the truthful charges of Mr. Brown published, employed the Rev. Dr. A. Bullard, a pro-slavery, negro-hating clergyman, formerly of the North, but now of St. Louis, to refute the charge; which the Doctor attempted to do, in a series of articles published in the columns of Northern pro-slavery papers of his own denomination. But the Presbyterian D. D., instead of mending the matter for his patron, made it worse, and caused the public to regard himself as a miserable tool. Mr. Page has since failed in his banking business, and swindled his creditors out of large sums; and has no doubt lost the misplaced confidence of his renegade theological friend.

Haskell, the overseer, experienced religion about this time, and joined the Duncards, a religious sect located at the Southwest, who baptise by immersion, dipping their converts three times. The overseer being an unprincipled scamp, noted for his drinking propensities, and for cheating all with whom he dealt, a large number of persons assembled to witness the baptismal ceremony performed on the negro-driver. Some of the blacks are very superstitious, and are of opinion that the Lord will answer their prayers, in any case when they ask for the extermination of bad men. So, the day that the overseer was led to the pond to have his sins washed out, not less than nine of the oldest slaves went on their knees, and prayed that the cruel negro-driver might not come out of the water alive. Among the crowd that had come together was old Peter Swite, who kept a dram shop, and who complained that Haskell owed him several dollars for drink, but which the overseer denied. As John Mason, the minister, pulled the negro-driver up, after dipping him the third time, old Peter took his pipe from his mouth, and cried out, at the top of his voice, "Douce him again, John! He's a dirty dog; I know him well; he never pays his debts." So the minister, either forgetting himself, or really thinking his new convert needed the fourth dip, put the sinner once more under the water. This last plunge came near drowning him, for the man of God was much exhausted, and was scarcely able to lift the negro-driver out of the water, and the latter had taken two or three hearty drinks before he was drawn to the surface. Although the prayers of the slaves were not answered, they nevertheless took great credit to themselves for the misstep of the minister. That night, the slaves on the whole plantation were in the highest glee. The opossums that had been lying in the frost were taken down and baked with sweet potatoes, and every voice ascended to God, either in prayer or in song, for the half success of their prayers at the baptism.

# VII

*"Give me my child!" a mother cried,*
*"My sweet, my lovely boy—*
*("Give me my child!" the rocks replied)—*
*Or else my life destroy!"*

Want of money induced Dr. Young to hire William out again, and this time the young slave was placed in the hands of Walker, the negro-trader of whom we have made mention in a preceding chapter. The speculator had noticed William's activity and usefulness as a waiter on the steamboat, and being always on the look-out for valuable slaves, called on Dr. Young, and offered a high price for the piece of property. The Doctor, however, declined selling; whereupon, the trader, wanting a man to look after his slaves that he took to market, resolved to hire William for the period of one year, with the hope of buying him at the expiration of the term. Walker was an uncouth, ill-bred man, with little or no education. Before embarking as a negro-driver, he had been a dray-driver in St. Louis, and had earned, by his own hard labor, the capital with which he commenced in trade. Money was the only God he worshipped, and he knelt at no altar but that erected at the expense of suffering humanity. William shuddered at the idea of having such a man for a master, but there was no alternative.

In no situation could he have been placed to give him an opportunity of witnessing more scenes of cruelty and outrage than this. The trader had a number of slaves on hand, and immediately prepared to start with his human cattle for the New Orleans market. Between sixty and seventy men and women, chained in pairs, with here and there a mother with a young child unchained, made up the first coffle. The speculator advertised in the Natchez, Vicksburg and New Orleans papers, that he would be there at a given time, with a lot of healthy negroes, between fifteen and twenty-five years of age. He seldom, however, took down a gang of slaves without having some who were further advanced in years.

Soon after leaving St. Louis, William had to commence preparing the slaves for the market. The old men's gray hairs were plucked from their heads, and their whiskers shaved off clean; and where the white hairs were too numerous, hair dye was used to bring about the desired color. These old men and women were also told how old they were to be, when undergoing an examination by those who might wish to purchase.

Not less than four lots of slaves were purchased by this monster in human shape, and resold further South, during the year that William was with this "soul-driver." On the arrival of the trader at New Orleans with his merchandise, swarms of planters and small speculators might be seen making their way to Mr. Walker's slave-pen. Once, when marching his gang of slaves from St. Charles to St. Louis, by land, the trader had among them a woman, with a sick child, which cried during the most of the first day. Walker repeatedly told the mother if she did not stop the child, he would. On the second morning, as they were leaving the tavern where they had put up over night, the infant again commenced crying. The speculator at once took the child from its mother's arms, turned to the landlady, who was standing in the doorway, and said,—"Here, madam, permit me to present this little nigger to you; it makes such a noise that it affects my nerves." The landlady received the babe from the hands of the negro-trader with a smile, and said,—"I am exceedingly obliged to you, sir, indeed. I take this present as a token of your kindness and generosity." Frantic with grief, the mother fell upon her knees before the inhuman trader, and besought him to give her back her child, promising that she would keep it from crying. Walker bade the woman return to the gang with the other slaves, or he would flog her severely. But not until the heavy negro-whip was applied to her shoulders did the almost heart-broken mother leave her dear little child. A few days after, and while on the steamer going to the New Orleans market, this outraged American woman threw herself from the deck of the boat into the waters of the Mississippi, never to rise again.

This heartless, cruel, ungodly man, who neither loved his Maker nor feared Satan, was a fair representative of thousands of demons in human form that are engaged in buying and selling God's children. The more William saw of slavery, while with Walker, the more he hated it, and determined to free himself from its chains. The love of freedom is a sentiment natural to the human heart, and the want of it is felt by him who does not possess it. He feels it a reproach, and with this sting, this wounded pride, hating degradation, and looking forward to the cravings of the heart, the enslaved is always on the alert for an opportunity to escape from his oppressors and to avenge his wrongs. What greater injury and indignity can be offered to man, than to make him the bond-slave of his fellow-man?

## VIII

*"The hounds are baying on my track,*
*O, Christian! do not send me back!"*

After a year spent in the employment of the slave-driver, Walker, William was sent home to his master, where new scenes were opened to him. Although hard pressed for money, Dr. Young declined selling William to the slave-speculator, for he no doubt had some conscientious scruples against allowing his young kinsman to be taken to the cotton fields of the far South. He therefore gave his nephew a note, permitting him to find a purchaser who would pay five hundred dollars for him. With this document, the young slave set out for St. Louis, about four miles distant from the farm. Elizabeth, William's sister, who had been sold a few days previous, was still in the St. Louis jail; and on arriving in the city, his first impulse was to visit her, to whom he was tenderly attached. He called at the prison, and after being twice refused admission, succeeded in seeing his sister for the last time. She was sold to a slave-trader, and taken to the Southern market, and was never heard of again by William.

From the jail, the poor young slave went to his mother, and persuaded her to fly with him to Canada. With scarcely food enough for three days, William and his mother crossed the river one dark night, and started for a land of freedom, with no guide but the North Star. Again and again they looked back at the lights, as they wended their way from the city, not knowing whether they would succeed in their arduous undertaking, or be arrested and taken back. They well knew that the runaway slave could find no sympathy from the people of Illinois, and therefore did not travel during the day. Night after night did these two fugitives come out of their hiding-place, and with renewed vigor wend their way northward. No one can imagine how wearily the hours passed during the days they remained in the woods, waiting for night to overshadow them. Most truly has the poet entered into the slave's feelings, when he says,—

*"Star of the North! while blazing day*
*Pours round me its full tide of light,*
*And hides thy pale but faithful ray,*
*I, too, lie hid, and long for night."*

The anxiety of the fugitives may be conceived from the following remarks of Mr. Brown, in his published narrative:—"As we travelled towards a land of liberty, my heart would at times leap for joy; at other times, being, as I was, almost continually on my feet, I felt as though I could go no further. But when I thought of slavery, with its democratic negro-whips, its republican chains, its well-trained bloodhounds, its pious, evangelical slaveholders,—when I thought of all this American hypocrisy, false democracy and religion behind me, and the prospect of liberty before me, I was encouraged to press forward; My heart was strengthened, and I forgot that I was either tired or hungry."

But the fugitives were not destined to realize their hearts' fondest wishes. On missing the runaways, the slaveholders put advertisements in the St. Louis newspapers, which had an extensive circulation in Illinois, besides sending printed handbills, by mail, to the postmasters in the towns through which it was expected the fugitives would pass. On the tenth day, William and his mother determined to travel by day, thinking that they were out of the danger of being apprehended. They had, however, been on the road but a short time, when they were overtaken by three men and arrested. None but one who has been a slave, and made the attempt to escape, and failed, can at all enter into the feelings of the fugitive who is caught and returned to the doom from which he supposed he had escaped. William and his mother were carried back to St. Louis, and safely lodged in prison until their masters should take them out.

## IX

> *"Throw open to the light of day*
> *The bondman's cell, and break away*
> *The chains the State has bound on him!"*

As the slave becomes enlightened, and shows that he knows he has a right to be free, his value depreciates. A slave who has once ran away is shunned by the slaveholders, just as the wild, unruly horse is shunned by those who wish an animal for trusty service. The slave who is caught in the attempt to escape is pretty sure of being sold and sent off to the cotton, sugar, or rice fields of Georgia, or other slave-consuming States. Every thing is done to keep the slave in ignorance of his rights. But God has planted a spark in the breast of man, that teaches him that he was not created to be the slave of another. Truth is omnipotent, and will make its way even to the heart of the most degraded. How well has the author of the "Pleasures of Hope" portrayed the progress of truth!

> *"Where barbarous hordes on Scythian mountains roam,*
> *Truth, mercy, freedom, yet shall find a home;*
> *Where'er degraded nature bleeds and pines,*
> *From Guinea's coast to Siber's dreary mines,*
> *Truth shall pervade the unfathomed darkness there,*
> *And light the dreadful features of despair.*
> *Hark! the stern captive spurns his heavy load,*
> *And asks the image back that Heaven bestowed;*
> *Fierce in his eye the fire of valor burns,*
> *And, as the slave departs, the man returns."*

The truth which had broken in upon William's mind made him a dangerous person in the midst of the slave population of the South, and he scarcely hoped to find a home any where short of a cotton plantation. Dr. Young, as soon as he was informed that his slave had been caught, had him taken to the farm and well secured until he could sell him. A wish on the part of the Doctor to get a good price for William, induced him to conceal the slave's attempt to escape. This was very fortunate for William, for in a few days he was sold to Mr. Samuel Willi, a merchant in St. Louis. But William's mother was not so fortunate, for she was placed in the hands of the slave-trader, and carried to the slave market of New Orleans. How pathetically Mr. Brown has described the parting scene with his mother! "It was about ten o'clock in the morning," says he, "when I went on board the steamboat where my mother had been taken, with other slaves, bound for the lower country. I found her chained to another woman. On seeing me, she dropped her head upon her bosom, her emotion being too deep for tears. I approached her and fell upon my knees, threw my arms around her neck, and mingled my tears with hers, that now began to flow. Feeling that I was to blame for her being in the hands of the slave-speculator, I besought my mother to forgive me. With that generosity which was one of her chief characteristics, and that love which seldom forsakes a mother, she said,—'My child, you are not to blame. You did what you could to free me and yourself; and in this, you did nothing more than your duty. Do not weep for me. I am old, and cannot last much longer. I feel that I must soon go home to my heavenly Master, and then I shall be out of the power of the slave-dealer.' I could hear no more; my heart struggled to free itself from the human frame. The boat bell rang, as a signal for all who were not going with the boat to got on shore. Once more I embraced my mother, and she whispered in my ear,—'My child, we must now part, to meet no more on this side the grave. You have always said you would not die a slave; I beseech of you to keep this promise. Try, my dear son, to get your freedom!' The tolling of the bell informed me that I must go on shore. I stood and witnessed the departure of all that was dear to me on earth."

This separation of the mother from the son inspired the latter with renewed determination to escape; but this resolve he kept locked up in his own heart.

# X

> *"O, what is life if love be lost,*
> *If man's unkind to man?"*

While employed on board the steamer "Otto," where his new master placed him, William had his own feelings often lacerated, by seeing his fellow-creatures carried in large gangs down the Mississippi to the Southern market. These dark and revolting pictures of slavery frequently caused him to question the refinement of feeling and goodness of heart so bountifully claimed by the Anglo-Saxon, and, in the language of the poet, he would think to himself,—

> *"Say, flows not in the negro's vein,*
> *Unchecked and free, without control,*
> *A tide as pure, and clear from stain,*
> *As foods and warms the white man's soul?"*

Continued intercourse with educated persons, and meeting on the steamer so many travellers from the free States, caused the slave to feel more keenly his degraded and unnatural situation. He gained much information respecting the North and Canada, that was valuable to him in his final escape.

In his written narrative, Mr. Brown says,—"The anxiety to be a freeman would not let me rest day nor night. I would think of the Northern cities I had heard so much about,—of Canada, where many of my acquaintances had found a refuge from their tyrannical masters. I would dream at night that I was on British soil, a freeman, and on awaking, weep to find myself a slave.

> *'I would think of Victoria's domain,*
> *In a moment I seemed to be there;*
> *But the fear of being taken again,*
> *Soon hurried me back to despair.'*

Thoughts of the future, and my heart yearning for liberty, kept me always planning to escape."

After remaining more than a year the property of Mr. Willi, William was sold to Capt. Enoch Price, also a resident of St. Louis. This change was the turning-point in the young slave's life.

## XI

*"Give me liberty or give me death!"*

Capt. Price, who became the last purchaser of William, was the owner of several steamers, and a partner in a firm in St. Louis, engaged in the business of purchasing and shipping produce to the Southern States. The young slave had been with the Prices scarcely three months, when the family resolved upon a visit to New Orleans, and it was settled that William should accompany them, as a servant. In due time, Capt. Price, with his wife and daughter, attended by their new chattel, set out on their journey, in one of the Captain's boats, the steamer "Chester." The boat, instead of returning to St. Louis, took in a cargo at New Orleans for Cincinnati, and the Captain and his family concluded to extend their visit to the latter place. It was the middle of December when the boat left New Orleans, with a large number of passengers and a heavy load of freight. The Prices had some fears about bringing the slave to the frontiers of the free States, and Mrs. Price sounded William, to see if he had any thoughts about freedom. As a matter of course, the young slave expressed a wish to return to St. Louis as soon as possible, and seemed to dislike the idea of going to a free State. Well pleased with his seeming indifference about liberty, and not being able to dispense with his services, the family determined to take William to Cincinnati with them.

In due time, the boat arrived at the place of her destination, landed her passengers, and discharged her cargo. Twenty years ago, there was little or no anti-slavery feeling in the southern part of the State of Ohio. Few persons thought it wrong to catch a runaway slave and return him to his master, and a fugitive ran as much risk in attempting to escape through the Buckeye State, at that time, as he would in the adjoining State of Kentucky. William, however, had resolved to make the attempt, without any regard to consequences. In his published narrative he says:—
"During the last night that I served in slavery, I did not close my eyes a single moment in sleep. When not thinking of the future, my mind dwelt on the past. The thought of a dear mother, and an affectionate sister and three brothers, yet living under the dominion of whips and scourges, caused me to shed many tears. If I could have been assured

that they were dead, I should have felt satisfied. But I imagined I saw my mother in the cotton field, followed by the merciless task-master. I thought of the probability of my sister and brothers being in the hands of negro-drivers or speculators, subjected to all the cruelties that the hateful institution allows them to inflict; and these thoughts made me feel very sad indeed."

At last the trying moment came. It was the first day of January, 1834, when, without a shilling in his pocket, and no friend to advise him, William quitted his master's boat, and, taking the North Star for his guide, started for Canada. During fifteen nights did this half-clad, half-starved fugitive urge his weary limbs to carry him on towards a land of freedom. With regard to these eventful days, Mr. Brown says in his narrative,—"Supposing every person to be my enemy, I was afraid to appeal to any one, even for a little food, to keep body and soul together. As I pressed forward, my escape to Canada appeared certain, and this feeling gave me a light heart, for

> 'Behind I left the whips and chains,
> Before me were sweet Freedom's plains.'

While on my journey at night, and passing farms, I would seek a corn-crib, and supply myself with some of its contents. The next day, while buried in the forest, I would make a fire and roast my corn, and drink from the nearest stream. One night, while in search of corn, I came upon what I supposed to be a hill of potatoes, buried in the ground for want of a cellar. I obtained a sharp-pointed piece of wood, with which I dug away for more than an hour, and on gaining the hidden treasure, found it to be turnips. However, I did not dig for nothing. After supplying myself with about half-a-dozen of the turnips, I again resumed my journey. This uncooked food was indeed a great luxury, and gave strength to my fatigued limbs. The weather was very cold,—so cold, that it drove me one night into a barn, where I laid in the hay until morning. A storm overtook me when about a week out. The rain fell in torrents, and froze as it came down. My clothes became stiff with ice. Here again I took shelter in a barn, and walled about to keep from freezing. Nothing but the fear of being arrested and returned to slavery prevented me, at this time, seeking, shelter in some dwelling. Even when in this forlorn condition, I would occasionally find myself repeating—

> *'I'll be free! I'll be free! and none shall confine*
> *With fetters and chains, this free spirit of mine;*
> *From my youth have I vowed in my God to rely,*
> *And, despite the oppressor, gain freedom or die!'*

Dreary were the hours that I spent while escaping from America's greatest evil."

## XII

*"O, then, be kind, whoe'er thou art
That breathest mortal breath,
And it shall brighten all thy life,
And gild the vale of death."*

So fearful are the tyrants at the South that their victims will recognise themselves as men, that they will not permit them to have a double name. Jim, Peter, Henry, &c. &c., is all a slave is known by. The subject of this memoir was not an exception to this rule. When William was six or seven years old, Dr. Young, having no children of his own, adopted a nephew, a son of his brother Benjamin. This boy's name was William, also, and not wishing to have the two names confounded, orders were given that the colored nephew's name should be changed, and accordingly he was afterwards called "Sanford." This name William always disliked, and resolved that he would retake his former name should he succeed in escaping to Canada.

After having been fifteen days on his journey, and having passed three days without food, and, withal, suffering much from illness, William determined to seek shelter and protection. "For this purpose," says he, "I placed myself behind some fallen trees near the main road, hoping to see some colored person, thinking I should be more safe under the care of one of my own color. Several farmers with their teams passed, but the appearance of each one frightened me out of the idea of asking for assistance. After lying on the ground for some time, with my sore, frost-bitten feet benumbed with cold, I saw an old, white-haired man, dressed in a suit of drab, with a broad-brimmed hat, walking along, leading a horse. The man was evidently walking for exercise. I came out from my hiding-place and told the stranger I must die unless I obtained some assistance. A moment's conversation satisfied the old man that I was one of the oppressed, fleeing from the house of bondage. From the difficulty with which I walked, the shivering of my limbs, and the trembling of my voice, he became convinced that I had been among thieves, and he acted the part of the Good Samaritan. This was the first person I had ever soon of the religious sect called 'Quakers.'"

At the farm-house of this good man, where many a poor fugitive slave had before found a resting-place for his jaded feet, William was treated with the kindest care, until he was so far recovered as to resume his journey. The members of no religious society are more noted for their good works than the FRIENDS. They are distinguished for the kindness with which they always receive the runaway slave. Having, many years ago, as a religious society, condemned slavery, and disfellowshipped slaveholders, they occupy a position before the world that few other sectarian bodies can claim. Never before having met with whites to sympathise with him, and treat him as a man, William was overwhelmed with surprise at the interest the Quaker and his family took in him.

> *"How softly on the bruised heart*
> *A word of kindness falls,*
> *And to the dry and parched soul*
> *The moistening teardrop calls."*

When once more in a situation to travel, the good people began to fit out the fugitive with clothes, so that he would be in a better condition to reach the "other side of Jordan." The Quaker's name was WELLS BROWN; and finding that his guest had but one name, he gave the fugitive his name, as well as a covering for his body. So, when the runaway quitted the Quaker settlement, he left under the name of WILLIAM WELLS BROWN.

# XIII

*"Where'er a single human breast*
*Is crushed by pain and grief,*
*There I would ever be a guest,*
*And sweetly give relief."*

The kind and benevolent Quakers would gladly have given their fugitive guest a home during the remainder of the cold weather, but they were afraid of his being sought after and traced to their house by the man-hunters. After being supplied with clothes and some food, Mr. Brown again started on his journey towards Canada. Although assured by his friends that he could travel with a degree of safety in the day, the fugitive felt that the night was the best time for him, and therefore hid in the woods during the day, and journeyed when others were asleep. Soon after, he arrived at Cleveland, on the banks of Lake Erie. The mind can scarcely picture one in a more forlorn condition than was WILLIAM WELLS BROWN on reaching Cleveland. Besides having had nothing to eat for the forty-eight preceding hours, and travelling through the woods and marshes, and over the frozen roads, he had worn out his shoes and clothes, so that he made a sad appearance. The lake was partly frozen, so that vessels did not run, and all hope of crossing to Canada was at an end. Wearied by his long journey on foot, Mr. Brown did not feel himself able to go on by the way of Buffalo or Detroit, and he at once resolved to hunt up quarters, and remain in Cleveland until the opening of navigation on the lakes. With this determination, he visited every dwelling, until he found a man who offered to keep him if he would work for his board. Here he sawed wood, and performed all the labor required of him, for a shelter from the inclemency of the winter weather.

While working at this place, the fugitive found an opportunity to saw a cord of wood for another family, for which he received the sum of twenty-five cents. With one half of this money, he purchased a spelling-book, and with the other he bought candy, with which he hired his employer's little boys to teach him to read.

Some weeks after, Mr. Brown obtained a situation at the Mansion House, kept by Mr. E. M. Segar. But on all occasions, he held on to his spelling-book, keeping it in his bosom, so that it might be handy.

In this manner was the foundation laid for an education which has enabled him to be of use to his race.

While at Cleveland, Mr. Brown saw, for the first time, an anti-slavery paper. It was the Genius of Universal Emancipation, edited by Benjamin Lundy.

Instead of going to Canada, on the opening of navigation in the spring, he got a situation on board the steamer "Detroit." Here he worked during the season of 1834. But the fugitive was destined to undergo more hardships, for at the close of navigation, the captain ran away with the money, and Mr. Brown, with others, had to go without his pay. Added to this, he had married during the autumn, and had taken upon himself the duties and responsibilities of a husband.

Thus defrauded of the avails of his nine months' labor, the fugitive went in search of employment for the winter. The following extract from an article written by Mr. Brown will give some idea, of the success he met with:—"In the autumn of 1824, having been cheated out of the previous summer's earnings by the captain of the steamer in which I had been employed running away with the money, I was, like the rest of the men, left without any means of support during the winter, and therefore had to seek employment in the neighboring towns. I went to the town of Monroe, in the State of Michigan, and while going through the streets, looking for work, I passed the door of the only barber in the town, whose shop appeared to be filled with persons waiting to be shaved. As there was but one man at work, and as I had, while employed on the steamer, occasionally shaved a gentleman, who could not perform that office himself, it occurred to me that I might get employment here as a journeyman barber. I therefore made immediate application for work, but the barber told me he did not need a hand. However, I was not to be put off so easily, and after making several offers to work cheap, I frankly told him that if he would not employ me, I would get a room near to him, and set up an opposition establishment. This threat made no impression on the barber, and as I was leaving, one of the men who were waiting to be shaved said, 'If you want a room in which to commence business, I have one on the opposite side of the street.' This man followed me out, we went over, and I looked at the room. He strongly urged me to set up, at the same time promising to give me his influence. I took the room, purchased an old table and two chairs, got a pole with a red stripe painted around it, and the next day opened, with a sign over the door,—

'Fashionable Hair-Dresser from New York—Emperor of the West.' I need not add that my enterprise was very annoying to the 'shop over the way,' especially my sign, which happened to be the most extensive part of the concern. Of course, I had to tell all who came in that my neighbor on the opposite side did not keep clean towels, that his razors were dull, and, above all, that he had never been to New York to see the fashions. Neither had I! In a few weeks, I had the entire business of the town, to the great discomfiture of the other barber.

"At this time, money matters in the Western States were in a sad condition. Any person who could raise a small amount of money was permitted to establish a bank, and allowed to issue notes for four times the sum raised. This being the case, many persons borrowed money merely long enough to exhibit to the Bank Inspectors, then the borrowed money was returned, and the bank left without a dollar in its vaults, if, indeed, it had a vault about its premises. The result was, that banks were started all over the Western States, and the country flooded with worthless paper. These were known as 'wild-cat banks.' Silver coin being very scarce, and the banks not being allowed to issue notes for a smaller amount than one dollar, several persons put out notes from six to seventy-five cents in value. These were called 'shin-plasters.' The 'shin-plaster' was in the shape of a promissory note, made payable on demand. I have often seen persons with large rolls of these bills, the whole not amounting to more than five dollars. Some weeks after I had commenced business on my 'own hook,' I was one evening very much crowded with visitors, and while they were talking over the events of the day, one of them said to me,—'Emperor, you seem to be doing a thriving business; you should do as other men of business, issue your shin-plasters.' This, of course, as it was intended, created a laugh; but with me it was no laughing matter, for from that moment, I began to think seriously of becoming a banker. I accordingly went, a few days after, to a printer, and he, wishing to get a job of printing, urged me to put out my notes, and showed me some specimens of engravings that he had just received from Detroit. My head being already filled with the idea of a bank, I needed but little persuasion to set the thing finally afloat. Before I left the printer, my notes were partly in type, and I studying how I should keep the public from counterfeiting them.

"The next day, my 'shin-plasters' were handed to me, the whole amount being twenty dollars, and, after being duly signed, were ready for circulation. At first, my notes did not take well; they were too new, and viewed with a suspicious eye. But, through the assistance of my customers, and a good deal of exertion on my own part, my bills were soon in circulation; and nearly all the money received in return for them was spent in fitting up and decorating my shop. Few bankers get through this world without their difficulties, and I was not to be an exception. A short time after my money had been out, a party of young men, either wishing to pull down my vanity, or to try the soundness of my bank, determined to give it 'a run.' After collecting together a number of my bills, they came, one at a time, to demand other money for them; and I, not being aware of what was going on, was taken by surprise. As I was sitting at my table, strapping some new razors I had just got with the avails of my 'shin-plasters,' one of the men entered and said, 'Emperor, you will oblige me if you will give me some other money for these notes of yours.' I immediately cashed the notes with some of the most worthless of the 'wild-cat' money that I had on hand, but which was a lawful tender. The young man had scarcely left when a second appeared, with a similar amount, and demanded payment. These were paid, and soon a third came, with his roll of notes. I paid these with an air of triumph, though I had but half a dollar left. I now began to think seriously what I should do, or how I should act, provided another demand should be made. While I was thus engaged in thought, I saw a fourth man crossing the street, with a handful of notes, evidently my 'shin-plasters.' I instantaneously shut the door, and, looking out of the window, said, 'I have closed business for the day; come to-morrow and I will see you.' On looking across the street, I saw my rival standing in his shop door, grinning and clapping his hands at my apparent downfall. I was completely 'done Brown' for the day. However, I was not to be 'used up' in this way; so I escaped by the back door, and went in search of my friend who had first suggested to me the idea of issuing notes. I found him, and told him of the difficulty I was in, and wished him to point out the way by which I could extricate myself. He laughed heartily, and then said, 'You must do as all bankers do in this part of the country.' I inquired how they did, and he said, 'When your notes are brought to you, you must redeem them, and then send them out and get other money for them, and with the latter you can keep cashing your own shin-plasters.' This was a new idea to me. I immediately commenced putting in circulation the notes which I had just redeemed, and my efforts were crowned with so much success, that before I slept that night, my 'shin-plasters' were again in circulation, and my bank once more on a sound basis."

The next spring, Mr. Brown again found employment on the lake, and from this time until the winter of 1843, he held a lucrative situation on one of the lake steamboats. Having felt the iron of slavery in his own soul, the self-emancipated slave was always trying to help his fellow-fugitives, many of whom passed over Lake Erie, while escaping from the Southern States to Canada. In one year alone, he assisted sixty fugitives in crossing to the British Queen's dominions. Many of these escapes were attended with much interest. On one occasion, a fugitive had been hid away in the house of a noted Abolitionist in Cleveland for ten days, while his master was in town, and watching every steamboat and vessel that left the port. Several officers were also on the watch, guarding the house of the Abolitionist every night. The Slave was a young and valuable man, of twenty-two years of age, and very black. The friends of the slave had almost despaired of getting him away from. his hiding-place, when Mr. Brown was called in, and consulted as to the best course to be taken. He at once inquired if a painter could be found who would paint the fugitive white. In an hour, by Mr. Brown's directions, the black man was as white, and with as rosy checks, as any of the Anglo-Saxon race, and disguised in the dress of a woman, with a thick veil over her face. As the steamers bell was tolling for the passengers to come on board, a tall lady, dressed in deep mourning, and leaning on the arm of a gentleman of more than ordinary height, was seen entering the ladies' cabin of the steamer "North America," who took her place with the other ladies. Soon the steamer left the wharf, and the slave-catcher and his officers, who had been watching the boat since her arrival, went away, satisfied that their slave had not escaped by the "North America," and returned to guard the house of the Abolitionist. After the boat had got out of port and fairly on her way to Buffalo, Mr. Brown showed the tall lady to her state-room. The next morning, the fugitive dressed in his plantation suit, snapped his fingers at the stars and stripes, bade his native land farewell, crossed the Niagara river, and took up his abode on the soil of Canada, where the American bondman is free.

## XIV

*"The weakest and the poorest may*
*This simple pittance give,*
*And bid delight to withered hearts*
*Return again and live."*

Wm. Wells Brown early became a reader of the Liberator, Emancipator, Human Rights, and other papers, published daring the first stages of the Anti-Slavery discussion, and consequently took great interest in the movement intended to abolish the cruel system under which his own relations, in common with others that were near and dear to him, were held. As one of the pioneers in the Temperance cause, among the colored people in Buffalo, he did good service. He regarded temperance and education as the means best calculated to elevate the free people of color, and to place them in a position where they could give a practical refutation to the common belief, that the negro cannot attain to the high stand of the Anglo-Saxon. But Buffalo being a place through which many fugitives passed while on their way to Canada, Mr. Brown spent much time in assisting those who sought his aid. His house might literally have been called the "fugitive's house." As Niagara Falls were only twenty miles from Buffalo, slaveholders not unfrequently passed through the latter place attended by one or more slave servants. Mr. Brown was always on the look-out for such, to inform them that they were free by the laws of New York, and to give them necessary aid. The case of every colored servant who was seen accompanying a white person was strictly inquired into.

Mr. Brown's residence also became the home of Anti-Slavery agents, and lecturers on all reformatory movements. After investigating every phase of Anti-Slavery, he became satisfied that the course pursued by WM. LLOYD GARRISON and his followers was the best calculated to free the slave from his chains, and he has over since been an advocate of the doctrines put forth by the great pioneer of the Abolition cause.

## XV

*"Where'er a human voice is heard*
*In witness for the true and right,*
*Where'er a human heart is stirred*
*To mingle in Faith's glorious fight,*
*That voice revere, that heart sustain,*
*It shall not be to thee in vain!"*

Having some three months leisure time during the winter, Mr. Brown began, in the autumn of 1843, to speak on the subject of American Slavery. Not satisfied with merely gaining his own freedom, he felt it to be his duty to work for others; and, in the language of the poet, he would ask himself—

*"Is true freedom but to break*
*Fetters for our own dear sake,*
*And, with leather hearts, forget,*
*That we owe mankind a debt?*
*No! true freedom is to share*
*All the chains our brothers wear,*
*And with heart and hand to be*
*Earnest to make others free."*

With this feeling, he went forth to battle against slavery at the South, and its offspring, prejudice against colored people, at the North. Buffalo and its vicinity was at that time one of the worst places in the State, with the exception of New York city, for colored persons. Hatred to the blacks had closed all the schools against colored children, and the negro-pew was the only place in the church where the despised race were permitted to have a seat. Mr. Brown not only combatted this unnatural prejudice in Buffalo, but also in the surrounding towns. On one occasion, he visited the town of Attica, to give a lecture on slavery, and so great was the hatred to the negro, that after the meeting was over, he looked in vain for a place to lodge for the night. After visiting every tavern in the village, he returned to the vestry of the church, and, entering it, remained until morning. The night was a bitter cold one, and Mr. Brown walked the aisle from eleven at night till six the next morning. One year after, he lectured in the same place, and the little seed left there, twelve months before, had taken root, and Mr. Brown found more than one person willing to take him in.

If there is one thing at the North which seems more cruel and hateful than another, connected with American slavery, it is the way in which colored persons are treated by the whites. The withering influence which this hatred exerts against the elevation of the free colored people, can scarcely be imagined. Wherever the black man makes his appearance in the United States, he meets this hatred. In some sections of the country it is worse than in others. As you advance nearer to the slave States, you feel this prejudice the more. Twenty years ago, if colored persons travelled by steamboat, they were put on the deck; if by coach, on the outside; if by railway, in the Jim Crow car. Even the respectable eating saloons have been closed against colored persons. In New York and Philadelphia, the despised race are still excluded from most places of refreshment. To the everlasting shame of the Church, she still holds on to this unchristian practice of separating persons on account of their complexion. In the refined city of Boston, there was a church, as late as 1847, deeded its pews upon condition that no colored person should ever be permitted to enter them! Most of these churches have a place set off in the gallery, where the negro may go if he pleases. A New York D. D., while on a visit to England, some years since, was charged by a London divine with putting his colored members in the furthest part of the gallery. The American clergyman, with a long face and upturned eyes, exclaimed, "Ah! my dear brother, I think more of my colored members than I do of the whites, and therefore I place them in the top of the house, so as to get them nearer to heaven." CHARLES LENOX REMOND, during the many years that he has labored in the Anti-Slavery cause, has, in all probability, experienced greater insults and more hardships than any other person of color. To hear him relate what he has undergone, while travelling to and from the places of his meetings, makes one's blood chill.

This pretended fastidiousness on the part of the whites has produced some of the most ridiculous scenes. WILLIAM WELLS BROWN, while travelling through Ohio in 1844, went from Sandusky to Republic, on the Mad River and Lake Erie Railroad. On arriving at Sandusky, he learned that colored people were not allowed to take seats in the cars with whites, and that, as there was no Jim Crow car on that road, blacks were generally made to ride in the baggage-car. Mr. Brown, however, went into one of the best passenger cars, seated himself, crossed his legs, and looked as unconcerned as if the car had been made for his sole use. At length, one of the railway officials entered the car, and asked him what he was doing there. "I am going to Republic," said Mr. Brown. "You can't ride here," said the conductor. "Yes I can," returned the colored man. "No you can't," rejoined the railway man. "Why?" inquired Mr. Brown, "Because we don't allow niggers to ride with white people," replied the conductor. "Well, I shall remain here," said Mr. Brown. "You will see, pretty soon, whether you will or not," retorted the railway man, as he turned to leave the car. By this time, the passengers were filling up the seats, and every thing being made ready to start. After an absence of a few minutes, the conductor again entered the car, accompanied by two stout men, and took Mr. Brown by the collar and pulled him out. Pressing business demanded that Mr. Brown should go, and by that train; he therefore got into the freight car, just as the train was moving off. Seating himself on a flour barrel, he took from his pocket the last number of the Liberator, and began reading it. On went the train, making its usual stops, until within four or five miles of Republic, when the conductor, (who, by-the-by, was the same man who had moved Mr. Brown from the passenger car) demanded his ticket. "I have no ticket," returned he. "Then I will take your fare", said the conductor. "How much is it?" inquired Mr. Brown. "One dollar and a quarter," was the answer. "How much do you charge those who ride in the passenger cars?" inquired the colored man. "The same," said the conductor. "Do you suppose that I will pay the same price for riding up here in the freight car, that those do who are in the passenger car?" asked Mr. Brown. "Certainly," replied the conductor. "Well, you are very much mistaken, if you think any such thing," said the passenger. "Come, black man, out with your money, and none of your nonsense with me," said the conductor. "I won't pay you the price you demand, and that's the end of it," said Mr. Brown. "Don't you intend paying your fare?" inquired the conductor. "Yes," replied the colored man; "but I won't pay you a dollar and a quarter." "What do you intend to pay, then?" demanded the official. "I will pay what's right, but I don't intend to give you all that sum." "Well, then," said the conductor, "as you have had to ride in the freight car, give me one dollar and you may go." "I won't do any such thing," returned Mr. Brown. "Why won't you?" inquired the railway man. "If I had come in the passenger car, I would have paid as much as others do; but I won't ride up here on a flour barrel, and pay you a dollar." "You think yourself as good as white people, I suppose?" said the conductor; and his eyes flashed as if he meant what he said. "Well, being you seem to feel so bad because you had to ride in the freight car, give me seventy-five cents, and I'll say no more about it," continued he. "No, I won't. If I had been permitted to ride with the other passengers, I would pay what you first demanded; but I won't pay seventy-five cents for riding up here, astride a flour barrel, in the hot sun." "Don't you intend paying any thing at all?" asked the conductor. "Yes, I will pay what is right." "Give me half a dollar, and I will say no more about it." "No, I won't," returned the other; "I shall not pay fifty cents for riding in a freight car." "What will you pay, then?" demanded the conductor. "What do you charge per hundred on this road?" asked Mr. Brown. "Twenty-five cents," answered the conductor. "Then I will pay you thirty-seven and a half cents," said the passenger, "for I weigh just one hundred and fifty pounds," "Do you expect to get off by paying that trifling sum?" "I have come as freight, and I will pay for freight, and nothing more," said Mr. Brown. The conductor took the thirty-seven and a half cents, declaring, as he left the car, that that was the most impudent negro that ever travelled on that road.

## XVI

*"For 'tis the mind that makes the body rich,*
*And as the sun breaks through the darkest clouds,*
*So honor peereth in the meanest habit."*

The subject of our memoir no sooner felt himself safe from the pursuit of the Southern bloodhounds, than he began to seek for that which the system of slavery had denied him, while one of its victims. During the first five years of his freedom, his chief companion was a book,—either an arithmetic, a spelling-book, a grammar, or a history. Though he never went through any systematic course of study, he nevertheless has mastered more, in useful education, than many who have had better privileges.

After lecturing in the Anti-Slavery cause for more than five years, Mr. Brown was invited to visit Great Britain. He at first declined; but being urged by many friends of the slave in the Old World, he at last, in the summer of 1849, resolved to go. As soon as it was understood that the fugitive slave was going abroad, the American Peace Society elected him as a delegate to represent them at the Peace Congress at Paris. Without any solicitation, the Executive Committee of the American Anti-Slavery strongly recommended Mr. Brown to the friends of freedom in Great Britain. The president of the above Society gave him private letters to some of the leading men and women in Europe. In addition to these, the colored citizens of Boston held a meeting the evening previous to his departure, and gave Mr. Brown a public farewell, and passed resolutions commending him to the confidence and hospitality of all lovers of liberty in the motherland.

Such were the auspices under which this self-educated man sailed for England on the 18th of July, 1849. Without being a salaried agent, or any promise of remuneration from persons either in Europe or America, the subject of our narrative arrived at Liverpool, after a passage of a few hours less than ten days.

## XVII

*"Erin, my country! o'er the swelling wave,*
*Join in the cry, ask freedom for the slave!"*

*"Natives of a land of glory,*
*Daughters of the good and brave,*
*Hear the injured negro's story,*
*Hear, and help the kneeling slave!"*

From Liverpool, Mr. Brown went to Dublin, where he was warmly greeted by the Webbs, Haughtons, Allens, and others of the slave's friends in Ireland. Her Brittanic Majesty visiting her Irish subjects at that time, the fugitive had an opportunity of witnessing Royalty in all its magnificence and regal splendor. The land of Burke, Sheridan and O'Connell would not permit the American to leave without giving him a public welcome. A large and enthusiastic meeting held in the Rotunda, and presided over by JAMES HAUGHTON, Esq., gave Mr. Brown the first reception which he had in the Old World.

After a sojourn of twenty days in the Emerald Isle, the fugitive started for the Peace Congress which was to assemble at Paris. The Peace Congress, and especially the French who were in attendance at the great meeting, most of whom had never seen a colored person, were somewhat taken by surprise on the last day, when Mr. Brown made a speech. "His reception," said La Presse, "was most flattering. He admirably sustained his reputation as a public speaker. His address produced a profound sensation. At its conclusion, the speaker was warmly greeted by Victor Hugo, President of the Congress, Richard Cobden, Esq., and other distinguished men on the platform. At the soirée given by M. de Tocqueville, the Minister for Foreign Affairs, the American slave was received with marked attention." More than thirty of the English delegates at the Congress gave Mr. Brown invitations to visit their towns on his return to England, and lecture on American Slavery.

Having spent a fortnight in Paris and vicinity, viewing the sights, he returned to London. GEORGE THOMPSON, Esq., was among the first to meet the fugitive on his arrival at the English metropolis. A few days after, a very large meeting, held in the spacious Music Hall, Bedford

Square, and presided over by Sir Francis Knowles, Bart., welcomed Mr. Brown to England. Many of Britain's distinguished public speakers spoke on the occasion. George Thompson made one of his most brilliant efforts.

This flattering reception gained for the fugitive pressing invitations from nearly all parts of the United Kingdom. At the city of Worcester, His Honor the Mayor presided over the meeting, and introduced Mr. Brown as "the honorable gentleman from America." In the city of Norwich, the meeting was held in St. Andrew's Hall, one of the oldest and most venerated buildings in the Kingdom, and the Chairman on the occasion was John Henry Gurney, Esq., the distinguished banker, and son of the late Joseph John Gurney. At Newcastle-on-Tyne, two meetings were held. His Honor the Mayor presided over one, and Sir John Fife over the other. Here the friends of freedom gave Mr. Brown a public soirée, at which eight hundred sat down to tea. After tea was over, the Mayor arose, and, on behalf of the meeting, presented to Mr. Brown a purse containing twenty sovereigns, accompanied with the following Address:—"This purse, containing twenty sovereigns, is presented to WM. WELLS BROWN by the following ladies and some other friends of the slave in Newcastle, as a token of their high esteem for his character and admiration of his zeal in advocating the claims of three millions of his brethren and sisters in bonds in the Southern States of America. They also express their sincere wish that his life may be long spared to pursue his valuable labors—that success may soon crown his efforts and those of his fellow-Abolitionists on both sides of the Atlantic, and his heart be gladdened by the arrival of the happy period when the last shackle shall be broken which binds the limbs of the last slave."

At Glasgow, four thousand persons attended the meeting at the City Hall, which was presided over by Alexander Hastie, Esq., M. P. Meetings given to welcome Mr. Brown were also held at Edinburgh, Perth, Dundee, Aberdeen, and nearly every city or town in the Kingdom. At Sheffield, James Montgomery, the poet, attended the meeting, and invited the fugitive to visit him at his residence. The following day, Mr. Brown went, by invitation, to visit the silver electro-plate manufactory of Messrs. Broadhead and Atkins. While going through the premises, a subscription was set on foot by the workmen, and on the fugitive's entering the counting-room, the purse was presented to him by the designer, who said that the donors gave it as a token of their esteem for Mr. Brown.

At Bolton, a splendid soirée was given to him, and the following Address presented:—

Dear Friend and Brother,

We cannot permit you to depart from among us without giving expression to the feelings which we entertain towards yourself personally, and to the sympathy which you have awakened in our breasts for the three millions of our sisters and brothers who still suffer and groan in the prison-house of American bondage. You came among us an entire stranger; we received you for the sake of your mission; and having heard the story of your personal wrongs, and gazed with horror on the atrocities of slavery, as seen through the medium of your touching descriptions, we are resolved henceforward, in reliance on divine assistance, to render what aid we can to the cause which you have so eloquently pleaded in our presence. We have no words to express our detestation of the crimes which, in the name of Liberty, are committed in the country which gave you birth. Language fails to tell our deep abhorrence of the impiety of those who, in the still more sacred name of Religion, rob immortal beings, not only of an earthly citizenship, but do much to prevent them from obtaining a heavenly one: and as mothers and daughters, we embrace this opportunity of giving utterance to our utmost indignation at the cruelties perpetrated upon our sex by a people professedly acknowledging the equality of all mankind. Carry with you, on your return to the land of your nativity, this our solemn protest against the wicked institution which, like a dark and baleful cloud, hangs over it; and ask the unfeeling enslavers, as best you can, to open the prison-doors to them that are bound, and let the oppressed go free. Allow us to assure you, that your brief sojourn in our town has been to ourselves, and to vast multitudes, of a character long to be remembered; and when you are far removed from us, and toiling, as we hope you may long be spared to do, in this righteous enterprise, it may be some solace to your mind to know that your name is cherished with affectionate regard, and that the blessing of the Most High is earnestly supplicated in behalf of yourself and family, and the cause to which you have consecrated your distinguished talents." (Signed by 200 ladies.)

In the spring of 1850, Mr. Brown was publicly welcomed at a large meeting held in the Broadmead Rooms, at Bristol, and presided over by the late JOHN B. ESTLIN, Esq., one of the most liberal-minded and philanthropic men of any country; a man who never appeared better satisfied than when doing good for others, and whose loss has been so universally lamented by the genuine friends of freedom in both hemispheres. But should we undertake to give a detailed account of the various meetings called to receive the American fugitive slave, it would occupy more space than we can think of giving in this volume.

# XVIII

*"'Tis a glorious thing to send abroad a soul as free as air,
To throw aside the shackles which sectarian bondmen wear."*

The following extract from Mr. Brown's "Sketches of Places and People Abroad," will show that all was not sunshine with him while in Europe. It was not the first time that forgetfulness for himself, and a desire to add to the comfort of others, placed him in an unpleasant position. The incident related below occurred during the first three months of the fugitive's sojourn in England:—

"Having published the narrative of my life and escape from slavery, and put it into the booksellers' hands, and seeing a prospect of a fair sale, I ventured to take from my purse the last sovereign, to make up a small sum to remit to the United States, for the support of my daughters, who were at school there. Before doing this, however, I had made arrangements to attend a public meeting in the city of Worcester, at which the Mayor was to preside. Being informed by the friends of the slave there, that I would, in all probability, sell a number of copies of my book, and being told that Worcester was only ten miles from London, I felt safe in parting with all but a few shillings, feeling sure that my purse would soon be again replenished. But you may guess my surprise when I learned that Worcester was above a hundred miles from London, and that I had not retained money enough to defray my expenses there. In my haste and wish to make up ten pounds to send to my children, I had forgotten that the payment for my lodgings would be demanded before I left town. Saturday morning came; I paid my lodging bill, and had three shillings and fourpence left. Out of this sum I was to get three dinners, as I was only served with breakfast and tea at my lodgings. Nowhere in the British Empire do the people witness such dark days as in London. It was on Monday morning in the fore part of October, as the clock on St. Martin's church was striking ten, that I I left my lodgings and turned into the Strand. The street lamps were all burning and the shop lamps were all lighted, as if day had not made its appearance. This great thoroughfare, as usual at this time of the day, was thronged with business men going their way, and women sauntering about for pleasure, or for want of something to do. I passed down the Strand to Charing Cross, and looked in vain to see the majestic statue of Nelson upon the top of the great shaft. The clock on St. Martin's church struck eleven, but my sight could not penetrate through the dark veil that hung between its face and me. In fact, day had been completely turned into night; and the brilliant lights from the shop windows, almost persuaded me that another day had not appeared. A London fog cannot be described. To be appreciated, it must be seen, or rather, felt, for it is altogether impossible to be clear and lucid on such a subject. It is the only thing which can give you an idea of what Milton meant when he talked of darkness visible. There is a kind of light, to be sure, but it only serves as a medium for a series of optical illusions, and for all useful purposes of vision, the deepest darkness that ever fell from the heavens is infinitely preferable. A man perceives a coach a dozen yards off, and a single stride brings him under the horses' feet; he sees a gas light faintly glimmering (as he thinks) at a distance, but scarcely has he advanced a step or two towards it, when he becomes convinced of its actual station by finding his head rattling against the post; and as for attempting, if you once get mystified, to distinguish one street from another, it is ridiculous to think of such a thing. Turning, I retraced my steps, and was soon passing through the massive gates of Temple Bar, wending my way to the city, when a beggar boy at my heels accosted me for a half-penny to buy bread. I had scarcely served the boy, when I observed near by, and standing close to a lamp-post, a colored man, and from his general appearance, I was satisfied that be was an American. He eyed me attentively as I passed him, and seemed anxious to speak. When I had got some distance from him, his eyes were still upon me. No longer able to resist the temptation to speak to him, I returned, and, commencing conversation with him, learned a little of his history, which was as follows:—He had, he said, escaped from slavery in Maryland, and reached New York; but not feeling himself secure there, he had, through the kindness of the captain of an English ship, made his way to Liverpool, and not being able to get employment there, he had come up to London. Here he had met with no better success, and having been employed in the growing of tobacco, and being unaccustomed to any other kind of work, he could not get labor in England. I told him he had better try to get to the West Indies, but he informed me that he had not a single penny, and that he had had nothing to eat that day. By this man's story I was moved to tears, and, going to a neighboring shop, I took from my purse my last shilling, changed it, and gave this poor fugitive one half. The poor man burst into tears, and exclaimed, 'You are the first friend I have met in London.' I bade him farewell, and left him with a feeling of regret that I could not place him beyond the reach of want. I went on my way to the city, and while going through Cheapside, a streak of light appeared in the east, that reminded me that it was not night. In vain I wandered from street to street, with the hope that I might meet some one who would lend me money enough to get to Worcester. Hungry and fatigued, I was returning to my lodgings, when the great clock on St. Paul's Cathedral, under whose shadow I was then passing, struck four. A stroll through Fleet street and the Strand, and I was again pacing my room.

"On my return, I found a letter from Worcester had arrived during my absence, informing me that a party of gentlemen would meet me the next day on reaching the place, and saying, 'Bring plenty of books, as you will doubtless sell a large number.' The last sixpence had been spent for postage stamps, in order to send off some letters to other places; and I could not even stamp a letter in answer to the last one from Worcester. The only vestige of money about me was a smooth farthing, that a little girl had given me at a meeting in Croyden, saying, 'This is for the slaves.' I was three thousand miles from home, with but a single farthing in my pocket! Where on earth could a man be more destitute for the want of money than in the Great Metropolis? The cold hills of the Arctic regions have not a more inhospitable appearance than London to the stranger with an empty pocket. But whilst I felt depressed at being in such a sad condition, I was conscious that I had done right in remitting the last ten pounds to America, for the support of those whom God had committed to my care. I had no friend in London to whom I could apply for aid. My friend Mr. T—was out of town, and I did not know his address. The dark day was rapidly passing away; the clock in the hall had struck six; I had given up all hopes of reaching Worcester the next day, and had just rung the bell for the servant to bring me some tea, when a gentle tap at the door was heard; the servant entered, and informed me that a gentleman below wished to see me. I bade her fetch a light, and ask him up. The stranger was my young friend, Frederick Stephenson, son of the excellent minister of the Borough-Road Chapel. I lectured in this chapel a few days previous, and this young gentleman, with more than ordinary zeal and enthusiasm for the cause of bleeding humanity and respect for me, had gone among his father's congregation and sold a number of copies of my book, and had come to bring me the money. I wiped the silent tears from my eyes, as the young man placed the thirteen half-crowns in my hand. I did not let him know under what obligation I was to him for this disinterested act of kindness. Like the man who called for bread and cheese, when feeling in his pocket for the last threepence with which to pay for it, found a sovereign that he was not aware he possessed, countermanded the order for lunch, and told them to bring him the best dinner they could get, so I told the servant, when she brought up tea, that I had changed my mind, and should go out to dine. With the means in my pocket of reaching Worcester the next day, I sat down to dinner at the Adelphi with a good cut of roast beef before me, and felt myself once more at home. Thus ended a dark day in London."

# XIX

*"Take the spade of perseverance,*
*Dig the field of progress wide,*
*Every bar to true instruction*
*Carry out, and cast aside."*

It was the intention of Mr. Brown, when he went to England, not to remain there more than one year at the furthest. But he was, by the laws of the United States, the property of another, and the passage of the Fugitive Slave Bill laid him liable to be arrested whenever he should return to his native land. WENDELL PHILLIPS, Esq., advised the fugitive, for his own safety, not to return. Mr. Brown therefore resolved to remove his two daughters to England, so that he could see to their education. In July, 1851, the girls arrived in Liverpool, in the Royal British Mail Steamer "America," under the charge of the Rev. CHARLES SPEAR, the distinguished and philanthropic friend of the prisoner. Even here, the fugitive was not without persecution in the person of his children, for Mr. Lewis, the Company's agent in Boston, would not receive them unless they were entered on the passenger's list as servants. The only reason assigned for this was their being colored! Thus the vile institution which had driven Mr. Brown into exile, followed his children on board a steamer over which the British flag waved.

Soon after the arrival of his daughters, Mr. Brown placed them in one of the best seminaries in France, where they encountered no difficulty on account of their complexion. The entire absence of prejudice against color in Europe is one of the clearest proofs that the hatred here to the colored person is solely owing to the overpowering influence of slavery. Mr. Brown's daughters, after remaining in France one year, were removed to the Home and Colonial School in London, the finest female educational college in Great Britain. Here, as well as in the French school, the girls saw nothing to indicate that the slightest feeling of ill-will existed on the part of the students towards them, because of their color.

## XX

*"Methinks I hear a tuneful voice
Chiming afar, o'er land and sea,
The sun of freedom wakes!—rejoice!
Thy bonds are broken—thou art free!*

In the winter of 1850, William and Ellen Craft, two fugitive slaves, arrived in England, and being in a strange land, and without the means of support, applied to Mr. Brown, who was just on the eve of making an anti-slavery tour through Scotland. Mr. Brown at once wrote to the Crafts to join him. These two interesting fugitives were born and brought up in Macon, Ga. To make their slaves more valuable, owners sometimes have them taught trades. A man who understands a good trade will sell for three or four hundred dollars more in the market. William Craft, having learned the trade of a cabinet maker, was able to earn considerable money for himself during hours when he was not required to work for his owner; and slaveholders always encourage their servants to labor, and get their own clothes, and other necessaries of life, because all that the slave gains in this way is so much saved by the master. William Craft did more than to get clothes for himself. In the course of five years, he laid aside one hundred and fifty dollars. William became acquainted with Ellen a slave girl owned by Dr. Collins, and residing in the same town. Like many of the slaves at the South, Ellen was as white as most persons of the clear Anglo-Saxon origin. Her features were prominent, hair straight, eyes of a light hazel color, and no one on first seeing the white slave would suppose that a drop of African blood coursed through her veins. With the permission of their owners, William and Ellen were united in marriage, after the fashion of the slaves. But both of these persons had long been lamenting their sad condition, and were only waiting for an opportunity of escaping from the house of bondage. It is usual, among what are called good slaveholders, to give their servants the Christmas week as a time of rest and pleasure. Such was the custom of the owners of William and Ellen. As the Christmas of 1848 approached, the Crafts, instead of studying how they should best spend their time in pleasure, began maturing a plan of escape. "I don't think this is a good half dollar," said William, as he finished counting his money late one night. "Still," continued he, "I shall have no trouble in passing it." "If some persons had your money, they would have a jolly time this Christmas," remarked Ellen. "I wish we could got our freedom with it," replied the husband. "Now, William," said the wife, "listen to me, and take my advice, and we shall be free in less than a month." "Let me hear your plans, then," said William. "Take part of your money and purchase me a good suit of gentlemen's apparel, and when the white people give us our holiday, let us go off to the North, instead of spending our time in pleasure. I am white enough to go as the master, and you can pass as my servant." "But you are not tall enough for a man," said the husband. "Get me a pair of very high-heeled boots, and they will bring me up more than an inch, and get me a very high hat, then I'll do," rejoined the wife. "But then, my dear, you would make a very boyish looking man, with no whiskers or moustache," remarked William. "I could bind up my face in a handkerchief," said Ellen, "as if I was suffering dreadfully from the toothache, and then no one would discover the want of beard." "What if you were called upon to write your name in the books at hotels, as I saw my master do when travelling, or were asked to receipt for any thing?" "I would also bind up my right band and put it in a sling, and that would be an excuse itself for not writing." "I fear you could not carry out the deception for so long a time, for it must be several hundred miles to the free States," said William, as he seemed to despair of escaping from slavery by following his wife's plan. "Come, William," entreated his wife, "don't be a coward! Get me the clothes, and I promise you we shall both be free in a few days. You have money enough to fit me out and to pay our passage to the North, and then we shall be free and happy." This appeal was too much for William to withstand, and he resolved to make the attempt, whatever might be the consequences.

Permission having been obtained from their master, William and Ellen went to spend their Christmas on Dr. Collins's farm, twelve miles from Macon. It was understood that the slaves were to start on their journey on the 24th of December, 1848, and to return to their employer on the day after Christmas. At the appointed time, instead of going to the farm, the husband and wife went to the railway depot, and took the six o'clock train for Philadelphia. Dressed in her new suit, with her hat of the latest fashion, and high-heeled boots, with a pair of spectacles, she had rather a collegiate appearance. Under the assumed name of William Johnson, she took her seat in a first-class car, while William, with his servant's ticket, entered the Jim Crow car. At Savannah, the fugitives took a steamboat for Charleston, and from thence, by railway and steamboat, they arrived at Philadelphia in four days. Many thrilling incidents occurred during their journey. At Charleston, Mr. Johnson stopped at the best hotel, and was not a little surprised to find himself seated near the Hon. John C. Calhoun at the dinner table. Both at Richmond and Washington, the fugitives came very near being detected. But the most amusing incident that happened during this novel journey was Mr. Johnson's making the acquaintance of a white family, who were also coming North. On the second day of the journey, a well-dressed old gentleman, accompanied by his two daughters, both unmarried, but marriageable, entered the car in which Mr. Johnson was, and took seats a short distance from him. The old gentleman, being rather communicative, soon entered into conversation with the young man in spectacles. "You appear to be an invalid," said the gray-haired gentleman, as he looked earnestly into the face of Mr. Johnson "Yes," replied the other, "I have long been afflicted with inflammatory rheumatism." "Ah! I know what that is, and can heartily sympathize with you," returned the old man. From the time of this conversation, both father and daughters appeared to take great interest in the young invalid. At every depot where they took refreshment, William acted his part as servant admirably. He waited on the old gentleman and his daughters, as well as on his own master, and by his politeness and attention attracted the notice of all. "That is a valuable servant of yours," said the old gentleman to Mr. Johnson, as William passed through the cabin of the steamer, while on the way from Savannah to Charleston. "Yes, sir, he is a boy that I am very much attached to," returned the young man. "Good negroes are valuable appendages," said the old man, yawningly, as he pulled his gold watch from his pocket to see the time. As the train approached Richmond, the old gentleman expressed great regret that they were to lose the company of their new acquaintance. "I am also sorry that we are to part," remarked Mr. Johnson. It was then discovered that Miss Henrietta, the oldest of the young ladies, seemed to have more interest in the young man than one would entertain for a mere acquaintance. "We are very much fatigued with this long journey," said the old gentleman, "and I am sure you must be tired; why won't you stop with us and rest yourself for a few days? My wife, knowing that you have been our travelling companion, will be glad to welcome you, and my daughter Henrietta here will be delighted." Miss Henrietta, feeling that this gave her an opportunity to speak, said, "Do, Mr. Johnson, stop and regain your strength. We have some pretty walks about Richmond, and I shall be so pleased to show them to you." The young invalid found that this was carrying the joke too far, and began to regret his intimate acquaintance with the young lady. However, he gave, as an excuse for declining the invitation, that urgent business demanded his immediate presence in Philadelphia, and promised them be would pay them a visit on his return to Georgia.

William and Ellen Craft, on their arrival in Philadelphia, committed themselves to the care of Mr. Brown, who was on a lecturing tour through Pennsylvania, and he brought them on to Boston. The Fugitive Slave Law drove them to England, where they again joined their old friend. Through Mr. Brown's influence, an interest was created for William and Ellen in England, and they were placed in a school, where they remained two years. In his "Sketches of Places and People Abroad," Mr. Brown describes an interview between Ellen Craft and Lady Byron as follows:—

"Some months since, a lady, apparently not more than fifty years of age, entered a small dwelling on the estate of the Earl of Lovelace, situated in the county of Surry. After ascending a flight of stairs and passing through a narrow passage, she found herself in a small but neat room, with plain furniture. On the table lay copies of the Liberator. Near the window sat a young woman, busily engaged in sewing, with a spelling-book lying open on her lap. The light step of the stranger had not broken the silence, so as to announce the approach of any one, and the young woman still sat at her task, unconscious that any one was near. A moment or two, and the lady was observed. The student hastily arose and apologized for her apparent inattention. The stranger was soon seated, and in conversation with the young woman. The lady had often heard the word 'slave,' and knew something of its application, but had never before seen one of her own sex who had actually been born and brought up in a state of chattel slavery; and the one in whose company she was now was so white, and had so much the appearance of a well-bred and educated lady, that she could scarcely realize that she was in the presence of an American slave. For more than an hour, the illustrious lady and the poor exile sat and carried on a most familiar conversation. The thrilling story of the fugitive slave often brought tears to the eyes of the stranger. O, how I would that every half-bred, aristocratic, slaveholding, woman-whipping, negro-hating woman of America could have been present and heard what passed between these two distinguished persons!

They would for once have soon one who, though moving in the most elevated and aristocratic society of Europe, felt it an honor to enter the small cottage, and take a seat by the side of a poor hunted and exiled American fugitive slave."

# XXI

*—"Yet press on!*
*For it shall make you mighty among men;*
*And from the eyrie of your eagle thought,*
*You shall look down on monarchs!"*

In 1852, Mr. Brown found, from the shortness of the lecturing season, which in England lasts only from November to May, and its furnishing a precarious means of living, that he must adopt some other mode of providing support for himself and his daughters, and therefore, through the solicitation of some of his literary friends, commenced writing for the English press. Not having received a classical education, he had often to re-write his articles. His contributions were mainly on American questions. For instance, his articles on the death of Henry Clay, Daniel Webster, the return of Anthony Burns, were gladly received by the London press, and the fugitive was liberally paid for his labors. The writer of this has known Mr. Brown to be engaged all night, after the arrival of an American mail, in writing for a morning newspaper. In the autumn of 1852, he published his "Three Years in Europe," which paid him well. The criticisms on this work brought the fugitive prominently before the public, and gave him a position among literary men never before enjoyed by any colored American. The London Morning Advertiser, in its review, said:—"This remarkable book of a remarkable man cannot fail to add to the practical protests already entered in Britain against the absolute bondage of three millions of our fellow-creatures. The impressions of a self-educated son of slavery, here set forth, must hasten the period when the senseless and impious denial of common claims to a common humanity, on the score of color, shall be scouted with scorn in every civilized and Christian country. And when this shall be attained, among the means of destruction of the hideous abomination, his compatriots will remember with respect and gratitude the doings and sayings of William Wells Brown. The volume consists of a sufficient variety of scenes, persons, arguments, inferences, speculations and opinions, to satisfy and amuse the most exigeant of those who read pour se desennuyer; while those who look deeper into things, and view with anxious hope the progress of nations and of mankind, will feel that the good cause of humanity and freedom, of

Christianity, enlightenment and brotherhood, cannot fail to be served by such a book as this."

The London Literary Gazette, in speaking of the book, remarked:—"The appearance of this book is too remarkable a literary event to pass without a notice. At the moment when attention in this country is directed to the state of the colored people in America, the book appears with additional advantage; if nothing else were attained by its publication, it is well to have another proof of the capability of the negro intellect. Altogether, Mr. Brown has written a pleasing and amusing volume, and we are glad to bear this testimony to the literary merit of a work by a negro author."

"That a man," said the Morning Chronicle, "who was a slave for the first twenty years of his life, and who has never had a day's schooling, should produce such a book as this, cannot but astonish those who speak disparagingly of the African race."

The London Critic pronounced it a "pleasingly and well written book." "It is," said the Athenæum, "racy and amusing," The Eclectic Review, in its long criticism, has the following:—"The extraordinary excitement produced by 'Uncle Tom's Cabin' will, we hope, prepare the public of Great Britain and America for this lively book of travels by a real fugitive slave. Though he never had a day's schooling in his life, he has produced a literary work not unworthy of a highly educated gentleman. Our readers will find in these letters much instruction, not a little entertainment, and the beatings of a manly heart on behalf of a down-trodden race, with which they will not fail to sympathize."

The British Banner, edited by Dr. Campbell, said:—"We have read this book with an unusual measure of interest. Seldom, indeed, have we met with any thing more captivating. It somehow happens that all these fugitive slaves are persons of superior talents. The pith of the volume consists in narratives of voyages and journeys made by the author in England, Scotland, Ireland and France; and we can assure our readers that Mr. Brown has travelled to some purpose. The number of white men is not great who could have made more of the many things that came before them. There is in the work a vast amount of quotable matter, which, but for want of space, we should be glad to extract. As the volume, however, is published with a view to promote the benefit of the interesting fugitive, we deem it better to give a general opinion, by which curiosity may be whetted, than to gratify it by large citation.

A book more worth the money has not, for a considerable time, come into our hands."

The Provincial papers and the London press united in their praise of this, the first literary production of travels by a fugitive slave. The Glasgow Citizen, in its review, remarked:—"W. Wells Brown is no ordinary man, or he could not have so remarkably surmounted the many difficulties and impediments of his training as a slave. By dint of resolution, self-culture and force of character, he has rendered himself a popular lecturer to a British audience, and vigorous expositor of the evils and atrocities of that system whose chains he has shaken off so triumphantly and for ever. We may safely pronounce William Wells Brown a remarkable man, and a fall refutation of the doctrine of the inferiority of the negro."

The Glasgow Examiner said:—"This is a thrilling book, independent of adventitious circumstances, which will enhance its popularity. The author of it is not a man in America, but a chattel,—a thing to be bought, and sold, and whipped; but in Europe, he is an author, and a successful one, too. He gives in this book an interesting and graphic description of a three years' residence in Europe. The book will no doubt obtain, as it well deserves, a rapid and wide popularity."

The Caledonian Mercury concludes an article of more than two columns of criticism and extracts as follows:—"The profound anti-slavery feeling produced by 'Uncle Tom's Cabin' needed only such a book as this, which shows so forcibly the powers and capacity of the negro intellect, to deepen the impression."

Mr. Brown's criticism on Thomas Carlyle brought about his ears a whirlwind of remarks from the friends of the distinguished Scotchman, while a portion of the press sided with the fugitive, and pronounced the article ably written and most just in its criticism. The following is the offensive part of the essay, and refers to his meeting Mr. Carlyle in an omnibus:—

"I had scarcely taken my seat, when my friend, who was seated opposite me, with looks and gestures informed me that we were in the presence of some disguised individual. I eyed the countenances of the different persons, but in vain, to see if I could find any one who, by his appearance, showed signs of superiority over his fellow passengers. I had given up the hope of selecting the person of note, when another look from my friend directed my attention to a gentleman seated in the corner of the omnibus. He was a tall man with strongly marked features, hair dark and coarse. There was a slight stoop of the shoulder,—that bend which is always a characteristic of studious men. But he wore on his countenance a forbidding and disdainful frown, that seemed to tell one that he thought himself better than those about him. His dress did not indicate a man of high rank, and had we been in America, I should have taken him for an Ohio farmer. While I was scanning the features and general appearance of the gentleman, the omnibus stopped and put down three or four of the passengers, which gave me an opportunity of getting a seat by the side of my friend, who, in a low whisper, informed me that the gentleman whom I had been eyeing so closely was no less a person than Thomas Carlyle. I had read his 'Hero Worship' and 'Past and Present,' and had formed a high opinion of his literary abilities. But his recent attack upon the emancipated people of the West Indies, and his laborious article in favor of the reestablishment of the lash and slavery, had created in my mind a dislike for the man, and I almost regretted that we were in the same omnibus. In some things, Mr. Carlyle is right; but in many, he is entirely wrong. As a writer, Mr. Carlyle is often monotonous and extravagant. He does not exhibit a new view of nature, or raise insignificant objects into importance; but generally takes common-place thoughts and events, and tries to express them in stronger and statelier language than others. He holds no communion with his kind, but stands alone, without mate or fellow. He is like a solitary peak, all access to which is cut off. He exists, not by sympathy, but by antipathy. Mr. Carlyle seems chiefly to try how he shall display his powers and astonish mankind by starting new trains of speculation, or by expressing old ones so as not to be understood. He cares little what he says, so that he can say it differently from others. To read his works is one thing—to understand them is another. If any one thinks that I exaggerate, let him sit for an hour over 'Sartor Resartus,' and if he does not rise from its pages, place his three or four dictionaries on the shelf, and say I am right, I promise never again to say a word against Thomas Carlyle. He writes one page in favor of reform and ten against it. He would hang all prisoners to get rid of them; yet the inmates of the prisons and workhouses are better off than the poor. His heart is with the poor; yet the blacks of the West Indies should be taught, that if they will not raise sugar and cotton of their own free will, 'Quashy should have the whip applied to him.' He frowns upon the reformatory speakers upon the boards of Exeter

Hall; yet he is the prince of reformers. He hates heroes and assassins; yet Cromwell was an angel, and Charlotte Corday a saint. He scorns every thing, and seems to be tired of what he is by nature, and tries to be what he is not."

# XXII

*"Fling out the anti-slavery flag,*
*And let it not be furled,*
*Till like a plant of the skies*
*It sweeps around the world!"*

Mr. Brown's name being often brought before the public through the reviews of his new book, and different sketches of his life having been published in the London Biographical Magazine, Public Good, True Briton, and other periodicals, he was invited to lecture before literary associations in London and the provincial towns. This induced him to get up a course of lectures on America and her great men, St. Domingo, &c. Thus, during the lecturing season, he was busily engaged, either before institutions, or speaking on American Slavery.

In the spring of 1853, the fugitive brought out his work, "Clotel, or the President's Daughter,"—a book of near three hundred pages, being a narrative of slave life in the Southern States. This work called forth new criticisms on the "Negro Author" and his literary efforts. The London Daily News pronounced it a book that would make a deep impression; while the Leader, edited by the son of Leigh Hunt, thought many parts of it "equal to any thing which has appeared on the slavery question."

Thus the fugitive slave slowly worked his way up into English literary society. After delivering a lecture before the London Metropolitan Athenæum, the Managing Committee instructed the Secretary to thank Mr. Brown, which he did in the following note:—

"Metropolitan Athenaeum, 189 Strand, June 21st
My Dear Sir,
   I have much pleasure in conveying to you the best thanks of the Managing Committee of this institution for the excellent lecture you gave here last evening, and also in presenting you, in their names, with an honorary membership of the Club. It is hoped that you will often avail yourself of its privileges by coming amongst us. You will then see, by the cordial welcome of the members, that they protest against the odious distinctions made between man and man,

and the abominable traffic of which you have been a victim. For my own part, I shall be happy to be serviceable to you in any way, and at all times be glad to place the advantages of the institution at your disposal."

"I am, my dear sir, yours, truly,"
William Strudwicke, Secretary
Mr. W. Wells Brown

Through Mr. Brown's influence and exertions, an Anti-Slavery meeting was hold on the First of August during the three last years of his residence in London.

The Morning Advertiser describes one of these occasions in the following terms:—

"It was on the First of August, that a number of men, fugitives from that boasted land of freedom, assembled at the Hall of Commerce, in the city of London, for the purpose of laying their wrongs, before the British nation, and, at the same time, to give thanks to, the God of freedom for the liberation of their West India brethren, on the First of August, 1834. At the hour of half past seven, for which the meeting had been called, the spacious hall was well filled, and the fugitives, followed by some of the most noted English Abolitionists, entered the hall, amid deafening applause, and took their seats on the platform. The appearance of the great hall at this juncture was most splendid. Besides the committee of fugitives, on the platform there were a number of the oldest and most devoted of the slave's friends. On the left of the Chair sat George Thompson, Esq., M. P., Sir J. Walmsley, Joseph Hume, Esq., M. P., and many other equally noted public men. Not far from the platform sat Sir Francis Knowles, Bart.; still further back was Samuel Bowley, Esq., while near the door were to be seen the greatest critic of the age, and England's best living poet. Macaulay had laid down his pen, entered the hall, and was standing near the central door, while not far from the historian stood the newly appointed Poet Laureate. The author of 'In Memorium' had been swept in by the crowd, and was standing with his arms folded, and beholding for the first time, and probably the last so large a number of colored men in one room.

The chair was most appropriately filled by Wm. Wells Brown, the distinguished fugitive slave from America. The Chairman first addressed the meeting in an eloquent and feeling manner, after which, speeches were made by Mr. George Thompson and others. The gathering was the most spirited one of the kind held in London for many years, and a good impression was made upon the assembled multitude."

No American visiting Great Britain ever had better opportunity of becoming acquainted with the condition of all classes of society than Mr. Brown. He saw every phase of life in England, Ireland, Scotland and Wales. He partook of the hospitality of the lord in his magnificent country-seat, and the peasant in his lowly cottage. A fashionable dinner is thus described by the fugitive in his "Sketches of Places and People Abroad":—

"It was on a pleasant afternoon in September that I had gone into Surrey to dine with Lord C—, and found myself one of a party of nine, seated at a table loaded with every thing that heart could wish. Four men-servants, in livery, with white gloves, waited upon the company. After the different courses had been changed, the wine occupied the most conspicuous place on the table, and all seemed to drink with a relish unappreciated except by those who move in the higher walks of life. My glass was the only one on the table into which the juice of the grape had not been poured. It takes more nerve than most men possess to enable one to decline taking a glass of wine with a lady; and in English society, they do not appear to understand how human beings can live and enjoy health without taking at least a little wine. By my continued refusal to drink, with first one and then another of the company, I had become rather an object of pity than otherwise. A lady of the party and in company with whom I had dined on a previous occasion, and who knew me to be an abstainer, resolved to relieve me from the awkward position in which my principles had placed me, and therefore caused a decanter of raspberry vinegar to be adulterated and brought on the table. A note in pencil from the lady informed me of the contents of the new bottle. I am partial to this kind of beverage, and felt glad when it made its appearance. No one of the party, except the lady, knew of the fraud, and I was able, during the remainder of the time, to drink with any of the company. The waiters, as a matter of course, were in the secret, for they had to make the change while passing the wine from me to the person with whom I drank. After a while, as is usual, the ladies all rose and left the room. The retiring of the fair sex left the gentlemen in a more free and easy position, and consequently, the topics of conversation were materially changed, but not for the better. The presence of ladies is always a restraint in the right direction. An hour after the ladies had gone, the gentlemen were requested to retire to the drawing-room, where we found tea ready to be served up. I was glad when the time came to leave for the drawing-room, for I felt it a great bore to be compelled to remain at the table three hours. Tea over, the wine was again brought on, and the company took a stroll through the grounds at the back of the villa. It was a bright moonlight night, the stars were out, and the air came laden with the perfume of sweet flowers, and there was no sound to be heard except the musical splashing of the little cascade at the end of the garden, and the song of the nightingale, that seemed to be in one of the trees near by. How pleasant every thing looked, with the flowers creeping about the summer-house, and the windows opening into the velvet lawn, with its modest front, neat trellis-work, and meandering vines! The small, smooth fish pond, and the life-like statues, standing or kneeling in different parts of the ground, gave it the appearance of a very Paradise. 'There,' said his lordship, 'is where Cowley used to sit under the tree and read.' This reminded me that we were near Chertsey, where the poet spent his last days; and, as I was invited to spend the night within a short ride of that place, I resolved to visit it the next day. We returned to the drawing-room, and in a few minutes after, the party separated."

Although mingling with some of the best men and women of Europe, Mr. Brown never forgot his country-men in bonds, or overlooked the fact that he was himself closely connected with them. Nor did his elevated position prevent his speaking out faithfully against the evils that degrade humanity in the old world. The temperance cause, peace, education, and the elevation of the laboring classes in Great Britain, claimed much of his time and attention.

During his residence abroad, Mr. Brown travelled more than twenty-five thousand miles through Great Britain, addressed above one thousand public meetings, and lectured before twenty-three literary societies, besides speaking at religious and benevolent anniversaries. Few persons could have accomplished more labor than did this fugitive slave during his five years' absence from America.

Mr. Brown rendered most valuable services to the cause of freedom while in England, by keeping on the track of every pro-slavery renegade who made his appearance there as an advocate of slavery. Rev. Dr. Prime,

Dr. Dyer, and others of the same way of thinking, found the fugitive at their heels wherever they went. He exposed them, held them up to the scorn and contempt of the people of Great Britain, through the columns of the English journals.

## XXIII

*"Ay, fettered not by creed, or clan, or gold, or land, or sea,*
*You roam through the world of light and life, rejoicing you are free."*

In the spring of 1854, a few ladies, personal friends of Mr. Brown, in England, wishing to secure to him the right of returning to the United States at any time that he might feel inclined, without the liability of being arrested as a fugitive slave, negotiated with his old master for the purchase of his freedom. As it may be interesting to the reader to know how an American disposes of his neighbors, we give below the Bill of Sale, called a Deed of Emancipation:—

"Know all men by these presents, That I, Enoch Price, of the city and county of St. Louis, and State of Missouri, for and in consideration of the sum of three hundred dollars, to be paid to Joseph Greely, my agent in Boston, Mass., by Miss Ellen Richardson, or her agent, on the delivery of this paper, do emancipate, set free, and liberate from slavery, a mulatto man named Sanford Higgins, alias Wm. Wells Brown, that I purchased of Samuel Willi on the 2d October, 1833. Said Brown is now in the fortieth year of his age, and I do acknowledge that no other person holds any claim on him as a slave but myself."

"In witness whereof, I hereunto set my hand and seal, this 24th day of April, 1854."

ENOCH PRICE
Witness, OLIVER HARRIS, JOHN K. HASSON

"STATE OF MISSOURI, COUNTY OF ST. LOUIS, s. s. In the St. Louis Circuit Court, April Term, 1854. April 25th.

"Be it remembered, that on this 25th day of April, eighteen hundred and fifty-four, in the open Court, came Enoch Price, who is personally known to the Court to be the same person whose name is subscribed to the foregoing instrument of writing as a party thereto, and he acknowledged the same to be his act and deed, for the purposes therein mentioned;—which said acknowledgment is entered on the record of the Court of that day.

In testimony whereof, I hereto set my hand and affix the seal of said Court, at office in the city of St. Louis, the day and year last aforesaid."

Wm. J. Hammond, Clerk.<br>
State of Missouri,<br>
County of St. Louis, S. S.

"I, Wm. J. Hammond, Clerk of the Circuit Court in and for the county aforesaid, certify the foregoing to be a true and correct copy of the Deed of Emancipation from Enoch Price to Sanford Higgins, (alias Wm. Wells Brown,) as fully as the same remains in my office.

"In testimony whereof, I hereto set my hand and affix the seal of said Court, at office in the city of St. Louis, this 25th day of April, eighteen hundred and fifty-four."

Wm. J. Hammond, Clerk.<br>
State of Missouri,<br>
County of St. Louis, S. S.

"I, Alexander Hamilton, sole Judge of the Circuit Court within and for the Eighth Judicial Circuit of the State of Missouri, (composed of the County of St. Louis,) certify that William J. Hammond, whose name is subscribed to the foregoing certificate, was at the date thereof, and now is, Clerk of the Circuit Court within and for the County of St. Louis, duly elected and qualified; that his said certificate is in due form of law, and that full faith and credit are and should be given to all such his official acts.

"Given under my hand, at the city of St. Louis, this 26th day of April, eighteen hundred and fifty four."

A. Hamilton, Judge

"July 7th, 1854. I have received this day Wm. I. Bowditch's check on the Globe Bank for three hundred dollars, in full for the consideration of the foregoing instrument of emancipation."

Joseph Greely,<br>
By Thomas Page's authority

The foregoing, reader, is true copy of the bill of sale by which a democratic, Christian American sells his fellow-countryman for British gold. Let this paper be read and the fact rung in the ears of our nervous negro aristocracy, who are upholding an institution which withers and curses the land, which blasts everything that it touches, which lies like an incubus on the nation's breast, which overshadows the Genius of the American Revolution, and makes our countrymen the scorn and by-word of the inhabitants of monarchical Europe.

# XXIV

> *"Hail, noble-hearted, sympathetic band!*
> *Men of hope-giving speech and ready hand!*
> *Followers of the Lowly One, who first began*
> *To plead for charity to fallen man!"*

As it regards social position, any government is preferable to that of the United States for a colored person to live under. The prejudice which exists in most of the American States against people of color is unknown in any European country. This, therefore, is a great inducement to colored Americans to take up their residence abroad. Although recognized as a man, and treated with deference by all he met, Mr. Brown wished to return to the United States. His feelings and inclinations were all with the slave and his friends, and his soul yearned to be where the great battle for freedom was being fought. With such feelings, he had no wish to remain in England, when informed by his friends that his liberty had been secured; he therefore made preparations to return home immediately. The following, from "Sketches of Places and People Abroad," will give some idea of the (now) freeman's feelings, when preparing for his departure from London:—

What a change five years make in one's history! The summer of 1849 found me a stranger in a foreign land, unknown to its inhabitants; its laws, customs and history were a blank to me. But how different the summer of 1854! During my sojourn, I had travelled over nearly every railroad in England and Scotland, and had visited Ireland and Wales, besides spending some weeks on the Continent. I had become so well acquainted with the British people and their history, that I had begun to fancy myself an Englishman, by habit, if not by birth. The treatment which I had experienced at their hands had endeared them to me, and caused me to feel myself at home wherever I went. Under such circumstances, it was not strange that I commenced with palpitating heart the preparations to return to my native land. Native land! How harshly that word sounds in my ears! True, America was the land of my birth; my grandfather had taken part in her Revolution, had enriched the soil with his blood, yet upon this soil I had been worked as a slave. I seem to hear the sound of the auctioneer's rough voice, as I stood on the block in the slave-market at St. Louis. I shall never forget the savage grin with which he welcomed a higher bid, when he thought he had received the last offer. I had seen my mother sold, and taken to the cotton-fields of the far South, three brothers had been bartered to the soul-drivers in my presence; a dear sister had been sold to the negro-dealer and driven away by him; I had seen the rusty chains fastened upon her delicate wrists; the whip had been applied to my own person, and the marks of the brutal driver's lash were still on my body. Yet this was my native land, and to this land was I about to embark."

Mr. Brown came home in the steamship "City of Manchester," and landed at Philadelphia, where a reception was given to him. "The meeting," says the Anti-Slavery Standard, "was held in the Brick Wesley Church, which was crowded to its utmost capacity with the friends of Mr. Brown, and the public generally, to extend to him the most cordial token of regard. The fact that he had faithfully and nobly represented his enslaved countrymen, while in Europe, was too obvious, in the estimation of those who had assembled to welcome and greet him on his return, to admit of a shadow of doubt. During the five years that Mr. Brown had passed in Europe, his numerous friends, especially the colored man, have had great cause of satisfaction and gratification in looking over his labors; as a lecturer, presenting the claims of his brethren in bonds; as an author, constantly using his pen in enlightening the British people on the monstrous iniquities of slavery, and likewise contributing to the demands of literature and knowledge in other respects—two of his works having been published and creditably noticed by the press of Great Britain."

ROBERT PURVIS, Esq., one of the most devoted friends of the slave, presided over the meeting, and at its close, the following resolutions were unanimously adopted:—"Resolved, That we rejoice in the opportunity afforded by this meeting of greeting our friend Wm. Wells Brown, on his return to this country, and that we hereby avail ourselves of it to extend to him our heartiest assurances of welcome.

"Resolved, That our thanks are due to Mr. Brown for the zeal and fidelity with which he has advocated the cause of freedom and the interests of the colored man in Great Britain, and that we are severally grateful to him for leaving a country where a black man labors under no disabilities, and where there is no prejudice against color, to return to this land of slavery, and labor for the disenthralment of his brethren from the hate of the white man and the chains of the slaveholder."

At Boston, a meeting was held in the Meionaon, at which FRANCIS JACKSON, Esq., the staunch friend of humanity, presided. Speeches were made by WM. LLOYD GARRISON, WM. C. NELL, and WENDELL PHILLIPS. The last-named speaker, in welcoming Mr. Brown, said,—"I rejoice that our friend Brown went abroad; I rejoice still more that be has returned. The years any thoughtful man spends abroad must enlarge his mind and store it richly. But such a visit is, to a colored man, more than merely intellectual education. He lives for the first time free from the blighting chill of prejudice. He sees no society, no institution, no place of resort or means of comfort from which his color debars him."

After mentioning some amusing instances of the surprise of Americans at this absence of prejudice abroad, Mr. Phillips said,— "We have to thank our friend for the fidelity with which he has, amid many temptations, stood by those whose good name religious prejudice is trying to undermine in Great Britain. That land is not all Paradise to the colored man. Too many of them allow themselves to be made tools of the most subtle foes of their race. We recognise, to-night, the clear-sightedness and fidelity of Mr. Brown's course abroad, not only to thank him, but to assure our friends there that this is what the Abolitionists of Boston endorse."

Mr. Phillips proceeded:—"I still more rejoice that Mr. Brown has returned. Returned to what? Not to what he can call his 'country.' The white man comes 'home.' When Milton heard, in Italy, the sound of arms from England, he hastened back—young, enthusiastic, and bathed in beautiful art as he was in Florence. 'I would not be away,' he said, 'when a blow was struck for liberty.' He came to a country where his manhood was recognised, to fight on equal footing. The black man comes home to no liberty but the liberty of suffering—to struggle in fetters for the welfare of his race. It is a magnanimous sympathy with his blood that brings such a man back. I honor it. We meet to do it honor. Franklin's motto was, Ubi Libertas, ibi patria—Where Liberty is, there is my country. Had our friend adopted that for his rule, he would have stayed in Europe. Liberty for him is there. The colored man who returns, like our friend, to labor, crushed and despised, for his race, sails under a higher flag: his motto is, 'Where my country is, there will I bring liberty!'"

## A Note About the Author

Josephine Brown (1839–1874) was an African American writer and youngest daughter of abolitionist and lecturer, William Wells Brown. She was raised in Massachusetts where she was educated, alongside her sister, at a boarding school. During her youth, Josephine would attend her father's many speaking engagements. She eventually joined him in his efforts as a teacher and antislavery lecturer. In an effort to preserve William's legacy, Josephine wrote *Biography of an American Bondman*, which was published in 1855.

## A Note from the Publisher

Spanning many genres, from non-fiction essays to literature classics to children's books and lyric poetry, Mint Edition books showcase the master works of our time in a modern new package. The text is freshly typeset, is clean and easy to read, and features a new note about the author in each volume. Many books also include exclusive new introductory material. Every book boasts a striking new cover, which makes it as appropriate for collecting as it is for gift giving. Mint Edition books are only printed when a reader orders them, so natural resources are not wasted. We're proud that our books are never manufactured in excess and exist only in the exact quantity they need to be read and enjoyed.

## Discover more of your favorite classics with Bookfinity™.

- Track your reading with custom book lists.
- Get great book recommendations for your personalized Reader Type.
- Add reviews for your favorite books.
- AND MUCH MORE!

Visit **bookfinity.com** and take the fun Reader Type quiz to get started.

Enjoy our classic and modern companion pairings!

Bookfinity is a registered trademark of Ingram Book Group LLC. © 2023 Bookfinity. All rights reserved.